D0515710

# Modern Fireplaces

Introduction   Ernst Danz
Examples   Axel Menges

Architectural Book Publishing Co. New York

Translation into English: Patricia Noris

Published 1979 in the U.S.A. by
Architectural Book Publishing Co., Inc., New York
All rights reserved
including the right of reproduction in whole
or in part in any form
Published simultaneously in Canada by
Saunders of Toronto, Ltd., Don Mills, Ontario
ISBN 8038–0165–3

© Copyright 1979 by Verlag Gerd Hatje, Stuttgart
Printed in Germany

## Contents

## Inhalt

1. Freestanding fireplace in a living room. Fireplace construction of aluminium. (Robert Wiley House, New Canaan, Connecticut, designed by Philip Johnson.)
2. Freestanding fireplace in a living room. Fireplace construction of steel plate. (Gerald Frey House, designed by H. Lovett.)
3. Fireplace incorporated in the external wall in a living room. Fireplace construction in natural-stone masonry. (Perlbinder Residence, Sagaponnack, New York, designed by Norman Jaffe.)
4. Freestanding fireplace in a living and dining room. Fireplace construction in masonry, plastered. (Casa Sert, Punta Martinet, Spain, designed by Josep Lluis Sert.)

1

2

## Preface

The open fireplace is not equally common in all countries. Statistical surveys have shown that Scandinavia, Great Britain and the USA have the largest distribution. Here we find the open fireplace not only in combination with other heating plants, which may be operated with coal, gas, oil or electricity, but also as sole heating source of a house, operated predominantly with wood, more seldom with coal. Moreover, fireplace heating here is by no means a privilege of comfortable dwellings alone. In other countries, however, the open fireplace is constructed almost exclusively for operation with wood and until a few years ago, its utilization was limited to single-family homes and vacation bungalows.

Today, heating technology has reached a stage almost beyond perfection. We need only consider the fully automatic air-conditioning plant and the various systems of local and central heating. Compared with the unquestionable superiority of such methods, the open fireplace cannot but lose its relevance to the technical aspects of heating. For all that, it does have an indisputable fascination which will most certainly secure its existence, even in the future. It is nevertheless important to take a realistic look at its function. The open fireplace today can no longer serve as principal domestic heating source, rather it has become a supplementary or transitional heating plant. Economically and in its efficiency it is in every way inferior to other heating methods. Its significance lies far more in the psychological effect. The dancing flames, the crackling of the wood and the smell of burning logs generate an atmosphere of relaxation, pensiveness and stimulation. The principal function of the fireplace today is to create a sphere of tranquility. In recollection of the earlier open hearth, grilling on an open fireplace has recently come back into fashion.

The open fireplace has not only in its external appearance become adapted to the formal conception of present-day architecture, but has also undergone a technical development which has succeeded in eliminating many of the earlier unavoidable shortcomings. Cold feet in front of the fire, biting smoke, unpleasant draughts and high fuel consumption are now things of the past. The results of intensive research work are no longer a firm secret, they form a reliable basis for the construction of perfectly functioning fireplaces. A large number of serial-type prefabricated fireplace units and complete fireplaces render possible low cost, uncomplicated installation. In addition, they guarantee maximal performance and functional reliability. With today's technical means, even those faults which, despite perfect construction, had eluded correction, may be eliminated. With this objective, for example, many experiments were undertaken to compensate depressions, katabatic winds and swirls with the aid of automatons, which simultaneously regulate the circulation velocity and preheat the smoke flue. Since the activity of the fire is by no means restricted by such fireplace robots, rather the combustion process is improved and the steering aggregate may be so accommodated that it remains outwardly invisible, there can hardly be any objections to such a perfect solution, if the technical expenditure and considerable costs are disregarded.

By an appropriate, restrained form and proper application of materials, many possibilities are offered for the external design of the open fireplace. Although the structural composition of the fireplace interior is subject to specific fundamental principles and regulations, a choice between various construction systems is given here also. However, only the expert can really decide which solution is more suitable in the particular situation. For this reason, planning and execution should also be entrusted to him, whereby the risk of disappointment is not entirely excluded, whether due to a minor constructive error or inaccurate workmanship. Sometimes however it is merely a small operational defect which mars the pleasure of the new fireplace. As consolation, it must be added that nearly every deficiency can be subsequently corrected when the actual cause has been traced. Hereby, the question of whether it is a case of a newly built fireplace or an improperly functioning old fireplace is of no importance.

The recurring query, whether one particular fireplace design is superior to another, can only be answered by means of a comparison in an efficiency scale. There would, however, be little sense in drawing up such a scale, since it would necessitate the inclusion of the most diverse construction systems (from the simple fireplace to the perfected high-power fireplace), in other words fireplaces subject to completely divergent conditions, and which cannot be placed with the same expectations. It is however by all means important that the fireplace be properly dimensioned and constructed with accuracy and expert knowledge. The technical data supplied by fireplace construction companies as well as research institutes, which fortunately coincide for the greater part, offer a valuable guide in the selection of the most suitable construction and at the same time constitute a reliable basis for the design. These particulars were also given due consideration in the theoretical introduction.

## Einleitung

Der offene Kamin ist nicht in allen Ländern gleich häufig vertreten; nach statistischen Untersuchungen weisen Skandinavien, Großbritannien und die USA die größte Verbreitung auf. Hier findet man den Kamin nicht nur in Verbindung mit anderen Heizungsanlagen, die mit Kohle, Gas, Öl oder elektrischem Strom betrieben sein können, sondern auch als einzige Heizquelle eines Hauses, und zwar vorwiegend mit Holz-, seltener mit Kohlenfeuerung. Außerdem ist die Kaminheizung hier keineswegs nur auf komfortable Wohnungen beschränkt. In den übrigen Ländern wird dagegen die offene Feuerstelle fast ausschließlich für die Holzverbrennung konstruiert, und bis vor wenigen Jahren baute man sie eigentlich nur in Einfamilien- oder Ferienhäusern ein.

Die Entwicklung der Heizungstechnik hat heute einen Stand erreicht, der an Perfektion kaum noch zu übertreffen ist. Man denke an die vollautomatisierte Klimaanlage oder an die verschiedenen Systeme der Lokal- und Zentralheizungen. Bei der eindeutigen Überlegenheit dieser Verfahren muß der offene Kamin zwangsläufig seine heiztechnische Bedeutung verlieren. Er hat jedoch unbestreitbare Reize, die ihm seine Existenz auch für die Zukunft sichern. Nur sollte man sich in bezug auf seine Verwendung von überholten Vorstellungen freimachen. Der offene Kamin kann heute nicht mehr die Hauptwärmequelle des Hauses sein, er ist vielmehr Zusatz- und Übergangsheizung geworden. In Wirtschaftlichkeit und Wirkungsgrad ist er anderen Heizverfahren in jedem Fall unterlegen. Seine Bedeutung liegt weit mehr in der psychologischen Wirkung. Der Anblick des Flammenspiels, das Knistern des Holzfeuers und der Geruch der brennenden Scheite erzeugen eine Atmosphäre der Entspannung, Besinnung und Anregung. Die Hauptaufgabe des Kaminbereichs ist heute, eine Zone der Ruhe zu bilden. In Erinnerung an das alte offene Herdfeuer kam in letzter Zeit auch wieder das Grillen im Kamin in Mode.

Der offene Kamin hat sich nicht nur in seiner äußeren Erscheinung den Formvorstellungen der Gegenwartsarchitektur angepaßt, sondern auch eine technische Entwicklung durchlaufen, die viele der früher unvermeidbaren Mängel beseitigen konnte. Kalte Füße vor dem Kamin, beißender Rauch, unangenehme Zugerscheinungen und hoher Brennstoffverbrauch gehören heute der Vergangenheit an. Die Ergebnisse intensiver Forschungsarbeiten sind kein Branchengeheimnis mehr, sie bilden eine zuverlässige Grundlage einwandfreier Kaminanlagen. Eine große Zahl serienmäßig vorgefertigter Kamineinsätze und Fertigkamine ermöglichen einen preiswerten, unkomplizierten Einbau. Sie garantieren außerdem ein Maximum an Leistung und Funktionssicherheit. Mit den heutigen Mitteln der Technik ist es durchaus möglich, selbst solche Störungen auszuschalten, denen bisher auch bei einwandfreier Konstruktion nicht beizukommen war. So hat man zum Beispiel Versuche unternommen, Flauten, Fallwinde oder Wirbel mit Hilfe von Automaten auszugleichen, die gleichzeitig für eine Steuerung der Strömungsgeschwindigkeit und die Vorwärmung des Rauchrohrs sorgen. Da die volle Entfaltung des Feuers auch bei solchen Kaminrobotern erhalten bleibt, der Verbrennungsvorgang eher noch verbessert und das Steuerungsaggregat so untergebracht werden kann, daß es von außen unsichtbar bleibt, ist gegen eine so perfektionierte Lösung kaum etwas einzuwenden, wenn man vom technischen Aufwand und den recht erheblichen Kosten absieht.

Die äußere Gestaltung des offenen Kamins bietet im Rahmen einer sinnvollen, beherrschten Formgebung und bei richtiger Materialverwendung sehr viele Möglichkeiten. Der innere, konstruktive Aufbau ist zwar bestimmten prinzipiellen Grundsätzen und Regeln unterworfen, doch gestattet auch er die Auswahl zwischen verschiedenen Konstruktionssystemen. Hier kann wirklich nur der Fachmann entscheiden, welche Lösung bei der jeweils gegebenen Situation die bessere ist. Ihm sollte man daher auch Planung und Ausführung überlassen. Das schließt nun allerdings nicht aus, daß es trotzdem einmal zu einer Enttäuschung kommen kann, sei es durch einen kleinen Konstruktionsfehler oder durch unsaubere Verarbeitung. Manchmal ist es aber auch nur ein kleiner Bedienungsfehler, der die Freude am neuen Kamin schwinden läßt. Zum Trost sei hier gesagt, daß sich fast alle Beanstandungen nachträglich beseitigen lassen, wenn die tatsächlichen Ursachen erkannt sind. Dabei spielt es keine Rolle, ob es sich um einen Kaminneubau oder um einen ungenügend funktionierenden alten Kamin handelt.

Die oft erhobene Frage, ob eine bestimmte Kaminausführung einer anderen überlegen sei, ließe sich nur durch die Gegenüberstellung in einer Leistungsskala beantworten. Es hätte jedoch wenig Sinn, eine solche aufzustellen, da sie die unterschiedlichsten Konstruktionssysteme (von der einfachen Feuerstelle bis zum perfektionierten Hochleistungskamin) umfassen müßte, Kamine also, bei denen völlig abweichende Voraussetzungen gegeben sind und an die nicht dieselben Erwartungen gestellt werden können. Wichtig ist jedoch in jedem Fall, daß die Konstruktion richtig dimensioniert und mit Sorgfalt und Sachkenntnis ausgeführt wird. Einen guten Ausgangspunkt für die Wahl der geeignetsten Konstruktion und zugleich eine sichere Basis für den Entwurf bilden die technischen Daten von Kaminbauunternehmen und Forschungsinstituten, die erfreulicherweise weitgehend übereinstimmen. Diese Unterlagen wurden auch in der theoretischen Einführung entsprechend berücksichtigt.

1. Frei stehender Kamin in einem Wohnraum. Kaminkonstruktion aus Aluminium. (Robert Wiley House, New Canaan, Connecticut, entworfen von Philip Johnson.)
2. Frei stehender Kamin in einem Wohnraum. Kaminkonstruktion aus Stahlblech. (Gerald Frey House, entworfen von Wendell H. Lovett.)
3. In die Außenwand eingebundener Kamin in einem Wohnraum. Kaminkonstruktion in Natursteinmauerwerk. (Perlbinder Residence, Sagaponnack, New York, entworfen von Norman Jaffe.)
4. Frei stehender Kamin in einem Wohn- und Speiseraum. Kaminkonstruktion in Mauerwerk, verputzt. (Casa Sert, Punta Martinet, Spanien, entworfen von Josep Lluis Sert.)

3

4

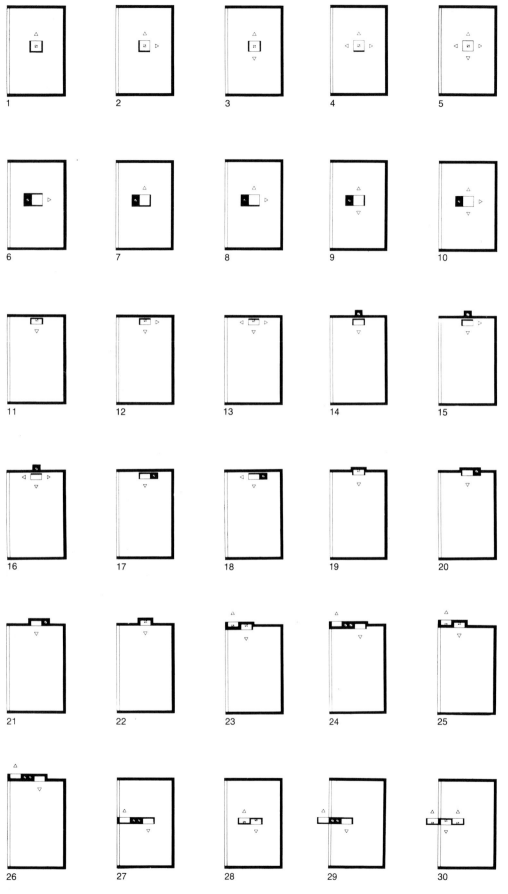

## Types of fireplace

A consequent list of open fireplace types, covering all items, should include the location, external structure and the structural composition. The alternate overlapping of many of the items would complicate a definition on this basis and the list of types, moreover, would be too extensive. For this reason, by omitting constructional details, the following classification was significantly reduced and the many types categorized in three groups. The plan sketches show a selection of varying basic conceptions; they were classified according to three factors: firstly, location or position of the fireplace, secondly, number of fireboxes and fireplace openings and thirdly, situation of the smoke flue or chimney in relation to the firebox.

1–10. Freestanding fireplaces. Location: as interior fireplace, freestanding in a room, in a corner, or in front of a wall; as external fireplace in a sheltered place, freestanding in the garden, or near the house. Firebox: one firebox; one, two, three, or four-sided (all-round) fireplace opening. Chimney: smoke flue or chimney above, at the side of, or behind the firebox.

11–22. Wall fireplaces. Location: as internal or external fireplace, flush with the wall, incorporated in the wall, hanging in front of the wall, arranged as fireplace wall or block. Firebox: one, two, or three-sided fireplace opening. Chimney: smoke flue or chimney above, at the side of, or behind the firebox.

23–30. Combination fireplaces. Location: as internal fireplace aligned to two areas or rooms, freestanding or incorporated in the room wall; as interior-exterior fireplace either in the room wall, as fireplace wall or block. Firebox: two, rarely three fireboxes, lying beside, behind, or in multi-storey buildings also above one another; one, two, or three-sided fireplace opening. Chimney as by freestanding and wall fireplaces.

31. Freestanding fireplace between two living rooms. (Simon Residence, Remsenburg, New York, designed by Julian Neski together with Barbara Neski and Ronald Bechtol.)

32. Fireplace forming a wall by itself in a living room. (Becker Residence, East Hampton, New York, designed by Norman Jaffe.)

33. Combination fireplace incorporated in an exterior wall with fireboxes in a family room (below) and a living room (above). (Kaplan Residence, East Hampton, New York, designed by Julian and Barbara Neski.)

## Kamintypen

Ein konsequentes, alle Positionen erfassendes Typenverzeichnis für offene Kamine müßte die Lage, das äußere Gefüge und den konstruktiven Aufbau einschließen. Die wechselseitige Überlagerung verschiedener Positionen kompliziert eine Definition auf dieser Basis, außerdem würde eine solche Typenliste zu umfangreich. Deshalb wurde die nachfolgende Gliederung durch den Verzicht auf konstruktive Einzelheiten wesentlich vereinfacht und die Vielzahl der Typen in drei Gruppen zusammengefaßt. Die Schemaskizzen zeigen eine Auswahl verschiedener Grundkonzeptionen; ihre Einordnung war durch drei Faktoren bestimmt: erstens durch Lage oder Standort des Kamins, zweitens durch die Anzahl der Feuerstellen und Feueröffnungen und drittens durch die Lage des Rauchrohrs oder Schornsteins in bezug auf die Feuerstelle.

31

1–10. Frei stehende Kamine. Lage: als Innenkamin frei im Raum, in einer Ecke oder vor einer Wand; als Außenkamin an einer windgeschützten Stelle frei im Garten oder in der Nähe des Hauses stehend. Feuerstelle: eine Feuerstelle; ein-, zwei-, drei-, vier- oder allseitige Feueröffnung. Schornstein: Rauchrohr oder Schornstein über, seitlich oder hinter der Feuerstelle.

11–22. Wandkamine. Lage: als Innen- oder Außenkamin wandbündig, eingebunden, vorgehängt, als Kaminwand oder -block angeordnet. Feuerstelle: eine Feuerstelle; ein-, zwei- oder dreiseitige Feueröffnung. Schornstein: Rauchrohr oder Schornstein über, seitlich oder hinter der Feuerstelle.

23–30. Kombinationskamine. Lage: als Innenkamin auf zwei Bereiche oder Räume ausgerichtet, frei stehend oder in der Raumwand; als Innen-Außenkamin entweder in Raumwand, als Kaminwand oder -block angeordnet. Feuerstelle: zwei, selten drei Feuerstellen, neben-, hinter- oder bei Mehrgeschoßbauten auch übereinanderliegend; ein-, zwei- oder dreiseitige Feueröffnung. Schornstein wie bei frei stehenden Kaminen und Wandkaminen.

31. Frei stehender Kamin zwischen zwei Wohnräumen. (Simon Residence, Remsenburg, New York, entworfen von Julian Neski mit Barbara Neski und Ronald Bechtol.)

32. Eine Wand bildender Kamin in einem Wohnraum. (Becker Residence, East Hampton, New York, entworfen von Norman Jaffe.)

33. In eine Außenwand eingebundener Kombinationskamin mit Feuerstellen in einem Familienraum (unten) und einem Wohnraum (oben). (Kaplan Residence, East Hampton, New York, entworfen von Julian und Barbara Neski.)

32

33

## Seating accommodation

The furniture in a separate fireplace room is always positioned in such a manner that the fireplace constitutes the focal point of the whole composition (advantage: clear orientation in the room, no penetration of functional areas). It is more difficult to create an appropriate relationship between fireside lounge group and fireplace when the latter is situated in the living room – as is usually the case. The separate fireside corner with additional seating is found relatively seldom; normally, one will attempt to make do with a single seating group (disadvantage: uncertain orientation, overlapping of functional areas). In this situation, it is advisable to consider first of all the normal living function of the furniture and then in the second instance its position to the fireplace, which is not always in operation and cannot therefore be the sole visual and reference point for the group seated around it. If the fireplace is not in use, the opportunity to look around the room, to look out into the open, into the adjoining room or at wall-shelves is preferable to having to stare into the soot-blackened hearth. Finally, the importance of suitable illumination of the seating area must not be forgotten. All these considerations can have a protracted influence on the location and construction of the fireplace and should be carefully taken into account in the earliest stages of planning. That in addition all seats must render a good view of the fireplace opening, goes without saying, just as does the necessity of adequate and if possible, even radiation of heat, to the chairs drawn back from the fireplace as well. As the adjacent diagrams show, a number of standard solutions have, in practice, crystallized, whereby it is necessary to distinguish between combinations of seating group and wall fireplace, corner fireplace or freestanding fireplace. Comfort will be the main factor in the choice of lounge groups. Stools and couches without backrests are no permanent alternatives. On the other hand, wing chairs, which best protect the back and neck from cold and draughts, are no longer in demand, since the fireplace is now predominantly used in combination with other heating systems. Preference should be given to leather or synthetic upholstery; textiles rapidly absorb the radiated warmth and store it.

1–6. Seating groups with side orientation to the fireplace. Advantage: view not limited exclusively to the fireplace. Disadvantage: seats at the distant end of the group receive less radiated warmth, for this reason seating is generally restricted to 4–6 places; improvement through armchairs without armrests or revolving armchairs (fig. 6). Favourable location of fireplace: in the external window wall or in the enclosing wall opposite.

7–15. Lounge groups with front orientation to the fireplace. Advantage: even radiation of heat, optimal view of the fireplace opening. Especially suitable for central fireplace openings and corner fireplaces (figs. 13–15). Disadvantage: fireplace obstructs field of vision; improvement through decoration of fireplace front (e. g. built-in wall shelves) or angular arrangement of seating accommodation (figs. 11, 12), the latter is only possible with a limited number of seats.

16–21. Circular or right-angled arrangement of chairs by central, freestanding fireplace with all-round open fire area. Advantage: relatively large number of seats, good utilization of heat. Disadvantage: more or less fixed orientation on the fireplace area, view blocked by the structural arrangement of the fireplace. Only suitable for especially large living areas or separate fireplace rooms. (Figs. 16, 17: layout of cushioned benches or sofas; fig: 18: armchairs arranged more loosely around the fireplace; figs. 19, 20: seat pits with circular or right-angled seating arrangement, cushioned seats and backrests; fig. 21: sunken fireplace surrounded by cushions lying on the room floor.)

22. Fireplace with side seating arrangement. (Monahan House, Castlecrag, Australia, designed by Harry Seidler.)

23. Fireplace with frontal seating arrangement. (Frisch Residence, Ashley Falls, Massachusetts, designed by Julian and Barbara Neski.)

24. Fireplace with circular seating arrangement. (Hiruzen Resort Lodge, Hiruzen Highlands, Japan, designed by the Takenaka Komuten Co., Ltd.)

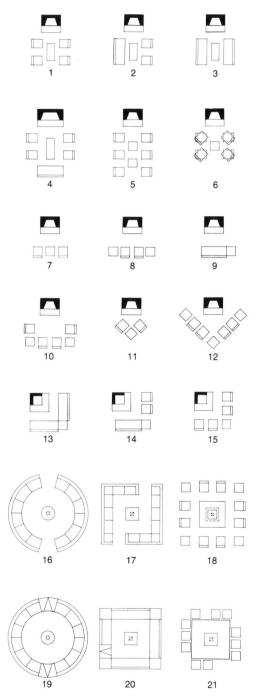

## Sitzgelegenheiten

Die Möblierung eines separaten Kaminzimmers wird immer auf den Kamin als Schwerpunkt ausgerichtet sein (Vorteil: eindeutige Orientierung im Raum, keine Durchdringung von Funktionsbereichen). Schwieriger ist es, im Wohnraum – wo der Kamin ja in den meisten Fällen steht – eine sinnvolle Beziehung zwischen Sitzgruppe und Kamin herzustellen. Die abgesonderte Kaminecke mit ausschließlich dafür bestimmten, zusätzlichen Sitzmöbeln ist relativ selten; normalerweise wird man mit einer einzigen Sitzgruppe auszukommen versuchen (Nachteil: mehrdeutige Orientierung im Raum, Überschneidung von Funktionsbereichen). In dieser Situation sollte man vernünftigerweise zunächst die normale Wohnfunktion der Sitzmöbel berücksichtigen und erst in zweiter Linie ihre Stellung zum Kamin, der ja nicht immer in Betrieb ist und deshalb auch nicht den einzigen Blick- und Bezugspunkt für die Sitzgruppe bilden kann. Ist er außer Betrieb, so möchte man nicht in das rußgeschwärzte Feuerloch starren müssen, sondern in den Raum oder in die freie Natur, ins Nachbarzimmer oder auf eine Regalwand sehen können. Nicht zu vergessen sind schließlich auch die Ansprüche, die an eine möglichst günstige Belichtung des Sitzbereichs gestellt werden dürfen. Alle diese Überlegungen können den Standort und die Gestaltung des Kamins nachhaltig beeinflussen und sollten daher schon im frühesten Planungsstadium angestellt werden. Daß zudem alle Plätze gute Sicht auf die Feueröffnung bieten müssen, versteht sich von selbst wie die Forderung nach ausreichender und möglichst gleichmäßiger Bestrahlung auch der abgerückteren Sitzgelegenheiten. Wie die nebenstehenden Zeichnungen zeigen, haben sich in der Praxis eine Reihe von Standardlösungen herausgebildet, wobei zu unterscheiden ist zwischen Kombinationen aus Sitzgruppe und Wandkamin, Eckkamin oder frei stehendem Kamin. Bei der Auswahl der Sitzmöbel wird man vor allem auf Bequemlichkeit sehen; Hocker und Liegen ohne Rückenlehnen bewähren sich auf die Dauer nicht. Andererseits aber ist auch der Ohrenbackensessel, der Rücken und Nacken am besten vor Zug und Kälte schützt, nicht mehr so gefragt, seit das Kaminfeuer hauptsächlich in Verbindung mit einem anderen modernen Heizsystem verwendet wird. Bei den Bezügen sollte man Leder oder Kunststoff den Vorzug geben, Textilien nehmen rasch die abgestrahlte Wärme auf und speichern sie.

1–6. Sitzgruppen mit seitlicher Orientierung zum Kamin. Vorteil: Blick nicht ausschließlich auf Kamin gerichtet. Nachteil: entferntere Sitze erhalten weniger Strahlungswärme, deshalb im allgemeinen Beschränkung auf 4–6 Plätze; Verbesserung durch Verwendung von Sesseln ohne Armlehnen oder Drehsesseln (Abb. 6.). Günstiger Standort des Kamins: in der Fensterwand oder in der gegenüberliegenden Umfassungswand.

7–15. Sitzgruppen mit frontaler Orientierung zum Kamin. Vorteil: gleichmäßige Wärmestrahlung, optimale Sicht auf die Feueröffnung. Besonders günstig bei mehrseitigen Feueröffnungen und Eckkaminen (Abb. 13–15). Nachteil: Kamin verstellt Blickfeld; Verbesserung durch gestalterische Maßnahmen an der Kaminfront (z. B. Einbau von Regalen) oder durch Schrägstellen der Sitzmöbel (Abb. 11, 12), letzteres ist nur bei beschränkter Platzzahl möglich.

16–21. Ringförmige oder rechtwinklige Anordnung der Sitzgelegenheiten bei zentralem, frei stehendem Kamin mit allseitig offenem Feuerraum. Vorteil: relativ viele Plätze, günstige Wärmeausnutzung. Nachteil: mehr oder weniger starre Bindung an den Kaminbereich, Sichtbehinderung durch den Kaminaufbau. Nur für besonders große Wohnräume oder spezielle Kaminzimmer geeignet. (Abb. 16, 17: Aufstellung von beweglichen Polsterbänken oder Sofas; Abb. 18: etwas lockerere Aufstellung von Einzelsesseln; Abb. 19, 20: ringförmig oder rechtwinklig angeordnete Sitzmulden, Sitz und Rückenlehne gepolstert; Abb. 21: Kamingrube, bei der die Sitzkissen auf dem Zimmerboden liegen.)

22. Kamin mit seitlich angeordnetem Sitzbereich. (Monahan House, Castlecrag, Australien, entworfen von Harry Seidler.)

23. Kamin mit frontal angeordnetem Sitzbereich. (Frisch Residence, Ashley Falls, Massachusetts, entworfen von Julian und Barbara Neski.)

24. Kamin mit ringförmig angeordnetem Sitzbereich. (Hiruzen Resort Lodge, Hiruzen Highlands, Japan, entworfen von Takenaka Komuten Co., Ltd.)

22

23

24

1, 2. Separate fireplace room with built-in furniture and massive partition wall with door to the living room. (Fig. 1: wall fireplace at an external wall; fig. 2: freestanding fireplace.)

3, 4. Fireplace area with built-in furniture, separated from the living area by a dividing element. (Fig. 3: wall fireplace at an external wall, shelf or cupboard wall as dividing element; fig. 4: freestanding fireplace block is combined with shelf wall to form a dividing element.)

5–8. Fireplace wall leading at right angles from an enclosing wall and projecting into the room, functions as room partition and divides the living space into two functional areas, here living and dining areas. (Fig. 8: combined interior and exterior fireplace in an exterior wall.)

9–12. Examples of utilization of freestanding fireplace blocks and walls. Visual separation of different areas here also. The fireplace unit is disengaged from the enclosing walls. (Figs. 11, 12: fireplaces with two fire openings, each aligned to a separate functional area.)

13. Freestanding fireplace which fits in well with the overall effect of the room.

14. Freestanding fireplace positioned more centrally, thus stronger accentuation on the fireplace area.

15–17. Wall-incorporated fireplaces are least conspicuous in the room, however they generally give rise to wall projections in the adjacent rooms or in the exterior wall. (Fig. 16: economical arrangement of two fireboxes, which are aligned to different rooms.)

18–24. Fireplaces set off sculpturally from an enclosing wall, in other words projecting fireplaces (figs. 18–22), effect a stronger accentuation of the fireplace area, as do wall-incorporated fireplaces (figs. 23, 24), and structure the wall space.

25, 26. Examples of fireplaces at open angles.

27, 28. Examples of fireplaces in projecting room corners.

29, 30. Exterior fireplaces. (Fig. 29: wall fireplace; fig. 30: freestanding exterior fireplace).

## Location

The determination of the most suitable location for the fireplace depends largely upon the orientation of the entire room structure (compare pages 10, 11). In the living room especially, it will be necessary to ensure that form and function of the neighbouring areas are not influenced by the all too imposing dominance of a fireplace. Consideration must also be given to the position of the chimney, which should either penetrate the fireplace structure at a suitable point or form an organic link with it.

The best solution is undoubtedly the provision of a separate fireplace room. Here, all technical and constructional requirements can be fulfilled without restriction and the room dimensions be proportioned according to the heating power of the fireplace. A similar situation is presented by a fireplace area separated from the living area by a bookcase wall or fireplace wall (frequently half-open or not quite flush with the ceiling). The absence of a door underlines the close relationship of the fireplace area to the living area. If the fireplace, as in most cases, is situated in the living room, the flush-with-the-wall arrangement is one of the most widely-used solutions. Outwardly, such a fireplace remains pertinent to the wall, so that utilization of the floor space is by no means restricted. Less conspicuous are fireplaces which project from an enclosing wall into the room. With the appropriate depth they function as room partitions, but even as flat projections they aptly break up the monotony of a too expansive wall surface. Corner fireplaces (installed diagonally or rectangularly) may be accommodated at open angles of approximately 90° or in projecting room corners. In the latter case, the disadvantage arising from the unprotected position between two functional areas, is compensated by the advantage of an equally good view of the fireplace opening at all angles. The all-round freestanding fireplace presupposes generous spatial dimensions, since by central arrangement the living room may otherwise be mistaken for a large fireplace room. On the other hand, the fireplace which stands completely free in the room offers (in single-family homes at least) the widest range of variation possibilities with regard to its location. Nevertheless, due consideration must be given to the fact that the freestanding fireplace, in particular in the form of a fireplace sculpture, dominates the room image and has in addition a more or less strong influence on the design of all other areas. Finally, reference must be made to the exterior fireplace, which if possible should be erected in a sheltered place – this also applies to the outdoor seating accommodation. Exterior fireplaces may be effectively combined with interior fireplaces provided they can be incorporated to the same wall.

If it is intended to accommodate several fireplaces (for example a second fireplace in the bedroom), the installation of a combined fireplace offers an economical solution without excessive constructional expenditure. If the chimneys are combined as a battery set, the fireboxes may be arranged superimposed on different floors or lying side-by-side and behind one another, whereby the fireplace openings face in the opposite direction.

16 17 18 19 20
21 22 23 24 25
26 27 28 29 30

1, 2. Separates Kaminzimmer mit Einbaumobiliar und massiver Trennwand mit Tür zum Wohnraum. (Abb. 1: Wandkamin an einer Außenwand; Abb. 2: frei stehender Kamin.)

3, 4. Vom Wohnraum durch Raumteiler abgetrennter Kaminbereich mit Einbaumobiliar. (Abb. 3: Wandkamin an einer Außenwand, Regal oder Schrankwand als Raumteiler; Abb. 4: frei stehender Kaminblock wird mit Regalwand kombiniert zum Raumteiler.)

5–8. Von einer Umfassungswand aus im rechten Winkel in den Raum greifende Kaminwand wirkt als Raumteiler und gliedert den Wohnraum in zwei Funktionsbereiche, hier Wohnen und Essen. (Abb. 8: kombinierter Innen- und Außenkamin in einer Fensterwand.)

9–12. Anwendungsbeispiele für frei stehende Kaminblöcke und -wände. Auch hier visuelle Trennung verschiedener Bereiche. Die Kamineinheit löst sich von den Umfassungswänden. (Abb. 11, 12: Kamine mit zwei Feuerstellen, die je auf einen Funktionsbereich ausgerichtet sind.)

13. Frei stehender Kamin, der sich in die Wirkung des Gesamtraums einfügt.

14. Frei stehender Kamin in mehr zentraler Anordnung, dadurch stärkere Betonung des Kaminbereichs.

15–17. Wandbündige Kamine treten im Raum am wenigsten in Erscheinung, ergeben jedoch meist Mauervorsprünge in den angrenzenden Räumen oder in der Außenwand. (Abb. 16: wirtschaftliche Anordnung zweier Feuerstellen, die auf verschiedene Räume ausgerichtet sind.)

18–24. Plastisch von einer Umfassungswand abgehobene, also vorgezogene Kamine (Abb. 18–22) setzen ebenso wie die in eine Raumwand eingebundenen Kamine (Abb. 23, 24) den Kaminbereich stärker ab und gliedern die Wandfläche.

25, 26. Beispiele für Kamine in offenen Winkeln.

27, 28. Beispiele für Kamine in vorspringenden Raumecken.

29, 30. Außenkamine. (Abb. 29: Wandkamin; Abb. 30: frei stehender Außenkamin.)

## Standort

Die Bestimmung des günstigsten Standorts für den Kamin hängt weitgehend von der Orientierung des gesamten Raumgefüges ab (vgl. Seiten 10, 11). Speziell im Wohnraum wird man darauf zu achten haben, daß Form und Funktion der angrenzenden Bereiche nicht durch die allzu starke Dominante eines Kamins beeinträchtigt werden. Natürlich ist auch die Lage des Schornsteins zu berücksichtigen, der entweder den Baukörper an einer günstigen Stelle durchdringen oder mit ihm eine organische Verbindung eingehen sollte.

Die beste Lösung ist zweifellos die Einrichtung eines separaten Kaminzimmers. Hier lassen sich alle technischen Voraussetzungen und gestalterischen Ansprüche uneingeschränkt erfüllen und die Raumabmessungen ganz auf die Heizleistung des Kamins abstimmen. Eine ähnliche Situation bietet der vom Wohnraum durch eine (oftmals halb offene oder nicht bis zur Decke reichende) Regal- oder Kaminwand abgetrennte Kaminbereich. Seine engere Zuordnung zum Wohnraum kommt auch im Verzicht auf eine Tür zum Ausdruck. Wird der Kamin, wie in den meisten Fällen, im Wohnraum eingebaut, so gehört die wandbündige Anordnung zu den weitaus häufigsten Lösungen. In der äußeren Erscheinung bleibt ein solcher Kamin der Wand zugehörig, die Bodenfläche steht also uneingeschränkt zur Verfügung. Weniger unauffällig sind Kamine, die von einer Umfassungswand aus in den Raum hineinragen. Bei entsprechender Tiefe wirken sie geradezu als Raumteiler, aber auch schon als flacher Vorsprung vermögen sie eine zu groß erscheinende Wandfläche geschickt zu gliedern. Eckkamine lassen sich (schräg oder rechtwinklig eingebaut) in offenen Winkeln von ungefähr 90° oder auch in vor-

springenden Raumecken unterbringen. Im letzteren Fall wird der Nachteil, den die ungeschützte Lage zwischen zwei Funktionsbereichen mit sich bringt, aufgewogen durch den Vorteil, daß sich die Feueröffnung aus den verschiedensten Blickwinkeln gleich gut übersehen läßt. Der allseits frei stehende Kamin setzt großzügige Raumabmessungen voraus, bei zentraler Aufstellung könnte der Wohnraum sonst wie ein großes Kaminzimmer wirken. Andererseits bietet der völlig frei im Raum stehende Kamin (wenigstens im Einfamilienhaus) die größten Variationsmöglichkeiten in der Standortfrage. Zu bedenken ist jedoch, daß der frei stehende Kamin, speziell in der Form einer Kaminplastik, das Raumbild weitgehend beherrscht und auch auf die Gestaltung der übrigen Bereiche einen mehr oder weniger starken Einfluß ausübt. Schließlich seien noch die Außenkamine erwähnt, die nach Möglichkeit an einer windgeschützten Stelle eingebaut werden sollten – eine Bedingung, die ja auch für die zugehörigen Freisitzplätze gilt. Außenkamine lassen sich sehr zweckmäßig mit Innenkaminen kombinieren, vorausgesetzt, daß es möglich ist, beide an der gleichen Wand anzuordnen.

Besteht die Absicht, mehrere Kamine unterzubringen (zum Beispiel eine zweite Feuerstelle im Schlafzimmer), so bietet sich der Einbau eines Kombinationskamins als wirtschaftlichste Lösung an, bei der kein übertriebener Aufwand erforderlich ist. Werden die Schornsteine zu einem Batteriesatz zusammengefaßt, so können die Feuerräume übereinanderliegend in verschiedenen Geschossen oder neben- und hintereinanderliegend angeordnet werden, wobei die Feueröffnungen in entgegengesetzte Richtung zeigen.

## Design

The possibilities for the formal design of the open fireplace are manifold. Depending on the desired effect, the frame of the hearth may be an inconspicuous element or a dominating, voluminous room sculpture. It should however be borne in mind that hearth and fireplace opening are the most important parts of the fireplace, and by all freedom of form, colour and material, the functional aspect of the individual parts must not be overlooked. Similarly, consideration should be given to the suitability of materials: it would for example be absurd to use metal plate for free-sculptural forms.

All fireproof and heatproof materials are suitable for the construction of the exterior fireplace mantle. Those most widely used are copper plate, iron plate, natural stones, hardburned profilated bricks and firebricks, concrete, ceramic tiles and various types of plaster finish. It is, however, important to determine whether a massive structure or mere facing is planned. In low-thickness materials, a solid substructure will be necessary, otherwise deformations or cracks may appear.

The simplest solution is undoubtedly the wall-incorporated fireplace, where only the fireplace opening is visible in the room. On the other hand, smoke hoods and prefabricated fireplaces, suspended on the wall, render a strong sculptural accent. Freestanding fireplaces generally constitute the dominating feature of the room.

It is often desirable to provide an additional focal point in the vicinity of the fireplace. Such combinations present a variety of interesting design alternatives. Shelves, built-in cupboards or a log bin may, for example, be accommodated in the fireplace wall; plant tubs, radios and television sets may be installed; a collection of objets d'art may be displayed in niches. Hereby, it is important to maintain a balance of values within the composition. Such decoration is more compatible with a simple wall fireplace than with a bold sculptural structure.

1. Freestanding fireplace serving as spatial divider in a living room. (Seidler House, Killara, Australia, designed by Harry Seidler & Associates.)
2. Fireplace incorporated in a parapet in a living room. (Frisch Residence, Ashley Falls, Massachusetts, designed by Julian and Barbara Neski.)
3. Freestanding fireplace on the terrace of a residential house. (House Z, Karlsruhe, designed by Reinhard Gieselmann.)
4. Fireplace forming part of a shelf and wood niche construction in a patio. (House in Cuernavaca, Mexico, designed by Karl-Heinz Götz.)

1

2

3

4

## Gestaltung

Die Möglichkeiten für die formale Ausgestaltung von Kamin und Kaminbereich sind denkbar vielfältig. Mit den verschiedenartigen Ausdrucksmitteln läßt sich sowohl ein unauffälliger Rahmen für die Feuerstelle als auch eine voluminöse Raumplastik von dominierender Wirkung schaffen. Man sollte jedoch immer davon ausgehen, daß Feuerstelle und Feueröffnung die wichtigsten Teile des Kamins sind. Bei aller Freizügigkeit in der Formgestaltung, Farbgebung und Materialwahl ist eben doch zu bedenken, daß es sich bei den einzelnen Teilen des Kamins um Funktionsglieder handelt. Ebensowenig sollte man die Frage der Materialgerechtigkeit außer acht lassen: es wäre zum Beispiel unsinnig, freiplastisch aufgebaute Formen in Blech ausführen zu wollen.

Als Baustoffe für den Außenmantel des Kamins kommen alle feuer- oder hitzebeständigen Materialien in Betracht. Am gebräuchlichsten sind Kupfer- und Eisenbleche, Natursteine, hartgebrannte Formsteine und Ziegel, Beton, Keramikplatten und verschiedene Putzarten. Man sollte aber berücksichtigen, ob eine massive Ausführung oder eine reine Verkleidung geplant ist. Bei geringer Materialstärke wird eine solide Unterkonstruktion erforderlich, da sonst Verformungen und Risse auftreten können.

Die einfachste Lösung sind zweifellos wandbündige Kamine, bei denen vom Raum her nur die Feueröffnung zu sehen ist. An der Wand aufgehängte Rauchschürzen und Fertigkamine bilden dagegen schon einen kräftigen plastischen Akzent. Frei stehende Kamine schließlich nehmen zumeist eine recht ausgeprägte Vorrangstellung im Raum ein.

Oft ist es wünschenswert, in der Nähe der Feuerstelle noch einen weiteren Blickpunkt zu schaffen. Aus derartigen Kombinationen ergeben sich viele weitere Gestaltungsmöglichkeiten. So lassen sich beispielsweise in der Kaminwand Regale, Einbauschränke oder die Holzlege unterbringen, es lassen sich Pflanzenwannen, Rundfunk- und Fernsehgeräte einbauen oder Nischen für Kunstgegenstände einrichten. Dabei ist ein Ausgleich der Werte Voraussetzung für eine überzeugende Lösung. Ein sehr plastisch gestalteter Kamin verträgt nun einmal solche Zugaben weniger als ein einfacher Wandkamin.

1. Frei stehender, der Raumgliederung dienender Kamin in einem Wohnraum. (Seidler House, Killara, Australien, entworfen von Harry Seidler & Associates.)
2. In eine Brüstung eingebundener Kamin in einem Wohnraum. (Frisch Residence, Ashley Falls, Massachusetts, entworfen von Julian und Barbara Neski.)
3. Frei stehender Kamin auf der Terrasse eines Wohnhauses. (Haus Z, Karlsruhe, entworfen von Reinhard Gieselmann.)
4. In eine Ablage- und Holzlegekonstruktion eingebundener Kamin in einem Wohnhof. (Haus in Cuernavaca, Mexiko, entworfen von Karl-Heinz Götz.)

## Dimensioning

The drawings opposite show, in diagrammatic representation, the structural composition of an open fireplace. They comprise the item symbols as they appear in the table of measurements, as well as other items not listed. In the explanation of the various items, all terminologies in common use and those applied in practice for one and the same structural detail are included. The drawings and table of measurements were prepared according to W. Häusler's *Cheminée-Handbuch* and a few items (FF and R in the table; device for ash removal in the drawing) have been added.

## Dimensionierung

Die nebenstehenden Zeichnungen zeigen in schematischer Darstellung den konstruktiven Aufbau eines offenen Kamins. Sie enthalten sowohl die in der Bemessungstabelle vorkommenden Positionsbezeichnungen als auch weitere, in der Tabelle nicht aufgeführte Positionen. Die Legende zu den verschiedenen Positionen führt alle für ein und dasselbe Konstruktionsdetail gebräuchlichen und in der Praxis verwendeten Begriffe auf. Die Zeichnungen und die Bemessungstabelle sind nach dem *Cheminée-Handbuch* von W. Häusler angefertigt und um einige Positionen (FF und R in der Tabelle; Aschenfallkonstruktion in der Zeichnung) erweitert.

*For heights of 8 to 12 m. Lower chimneys require larger cross-section.

*Für Höhen von 8 bis 12 m. Niedrigere Kamine erfordern größeren Querschnitt.

| Fireplace dimensions Kamin-Dimensionen | | | | | | | | Chimney size* Schornsteingröße* | | | Fireplace opening Feueröffnung | Room size Raumgröße |
|---|---|---|---|---|---|---|---|---|---|---|---|---|
| A cm | B cm | C cm | D cm | E cm | F cm | G cm | H cm | J cm | K cm | Calculated Berechnet cm² | FF cm² | R m³ |
| 60 | 50 | 30 | 40 | 30 | 20 | 13 | 12 | 20 | 20 | 300 | 3000 | 50 |
| 65 | 50 | 30 | 45 | 30 | 20 | 13 | 12 | 20 | 20 | 325 | 3250 | 60 |
| 70 | 55 | 30 | 45 | 30 | 20 | 13 | 12 | 20 | 20 | 385 | 3850 | 70 |
| 75 | 55 | 30 | 50 | 30 | 20 | 13 | 12 | 25 | 20 | 415 | 4125 | 75 |
| 80 | 60 | 35 | 55 | 30 | 20 | 13 | 12 | 25 | 20 | 480 | 4800 | 85 |
| 85 | 65 | 35 | 60 | 30 | 20 | 13 | 12 | 25 | 20 | 550 | 5525 | 100 |
| 90 | 70 | 40 | 60 | 30 | 20 | 13 | 12 | 25 | 25 | 630 | 6300 | 110 |
| 95 | 70 | 40 | 65 | 30 | 20 | 13 | 12 | 25 | 25 | 670 | 6650 | 120 |
| 100 | 75 | 45 | 70 | 30 | 20 | 13 | 12 | 30 | 25 | 750 | 7500 | 135 |
| 105 | 75 | 45 | 70 | 35 | 25 | 15 | 12 | 30 | 25 | 790 | 7875 | 140 |
| 110 | 80 | 45 | 75 | 35 | 25 | 15 | 12 | 30 | 30 | 880 | 8800 | 160 |
| 115 | 85 | 50 | 75 | 35 | 25 | 15 | 12 | 30 | 30 | 980 | 9775 | 175 |
| 120 | 85 | 50 | 80 | 35 | 25 | 15 | 15 | 35 | 35 | 1020 | 10200 | 185 |
| 125 | 90 | 55 | 85 | 35 | 25 | 15 | 15 | 35 | 35 | 1130 | 11250 | 205 |
| 130 | 90 | 55 | 90 | 35 | 25 | 15 | 15 | 35 | 35 | 1170 | 11700 | 210 |
| 135 | 95 | 55 | 90 | 35 | 25 | 15 | 15 | 35 | 35 | 1290 | 12825 | 230 |
| 140 | 100 | 60 | 95 | 35 | 25 | 15 | 15 | 40 | 40 | 1400 | 14000 | 250 |
| 145 | 100 | 60 | 100 | 35 | 25 | 15 | 15 | 40 | 40 | 1450 | 14500 | 260 |
| 150 | 105 | 65 | 100 | 35 | 25 | 15 | 15 | 40 | 40 | 1560 | 15750 | 280 |
| 155 | 110 | 65 | 105 | 40 | 30 | 15 | 15 | 40 | 40 | 1700 | 17050 | 305 |
| 160 | 110 | 70 | 110 | 40 | 30 | 15 | 15 | 40 | 40 | 1760 | 17600 | 315 |
| 165 | 115 | 70 | 110 | 40 | 30 | 15 | 15 | 40 | 40 | 1900 | 18975 | 340 |
| 170 | 120 | 75 | 115 | 40 | 30 | 15 | 18 | 40 | 40 | 2050 | 20400 | 370 |
| 175 | 120 | 75 | 120 | 40 | 30 | 15 | 18 | 40 | 40 | 2100 | 21000 | 380 |
| 180 | 125 | 75 | 120 | 40 | 30 | 15 | 18 | 50 | 50 | 2250 | 22500 | 405 |
| 185 | 125 | 75 | 125 | 40 | 30 | 15 | 18 | 50 | 50 | 2320 | 23125 | 420 |
| 190 | 130 | 80 | 125 | 40 | 30 | 15 | 18 | 50 | 50 | 2460 | 24700 | 440 |
| 195 | 130 | 80 | 130 | 40 | 30 | 15 | 18 | 50 | 50 | 2530 | 25350 | 455 |
| 200 | 135 | 80 | 135 | 40 | 30 | 15 | 18 | 50 | 50 | 2700 | 27000 | 485 |

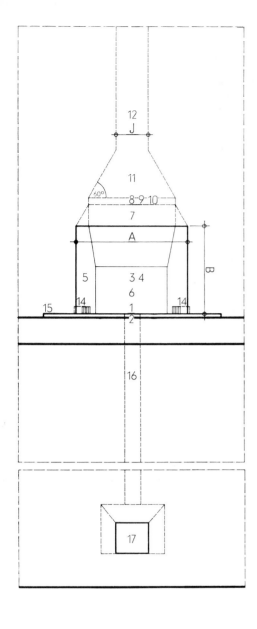

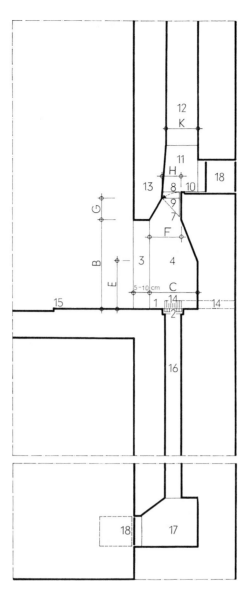

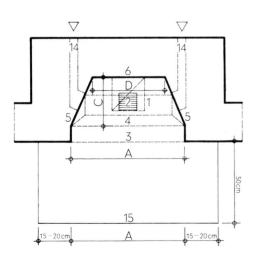

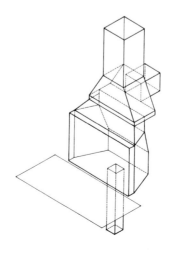

Key to table and diagrammatic drawing: A width of fireplace opening, B height of fireplace opening, C clear depth of firebox (total depth = C + 5–10 cm), D width of vertical back wall of firebox, E height of vertical back wall of firebox, F width of lower neck aperture, G height of neck, H width of upper neck aperture = width of throat, J clear width of smoke flue, K clear depth of smoke flue.

Key to the individual items (with alternative designations): 1 hearth, back hearth; 2 grate, ash grate; 3 fire opening, fireplace opening, radiation opening, fire aperture, hearth aperture; 4 firebox, fire area, hearth area, hearth; 5 firebox side-wall; 6 firebox back wall, hearth wall; 7 neck; 8 throat; 9 damper, throttle valve, regulating valve; 10 smoke shelf, down-draught shelf; deflection shelf; 11 smoke chamber, smoke collector; 12 chimney, smoke flue, chimney flue, smoke tube, smoke stack; 13 smoke apron, damper, chimney mantle, smoke hood, chimney hood; 14 supply-air duct, fresh-air duct, air duct; 15 safety area, foreplate, spark-arrest area; 16 ash dump, ash trap; 17 ash chamber, ash pit, cinder pit; 18 cleanout door, soot door.

Legende zu Tabelle und Schemazeichnung: A Feueröffnungsbreite, B Feueröffnungshöhe, C lichte Feuerraumtiefe (Gesamttiefe = C + 5–10 cm), D Breite der senkrechten Feuerraumrückwand, E Höhe der senkrechten Feuerraumrückwand, F untere Öffnungsbreite des Rauchhalses, G Höhe des Rauchhalses, H obere Öffnungsbreite des Rauchhalses = Breite der Rauchkehle, J lichte Breite des Rauchrohrs, K lichte Tiefe des Rauchrohrs.

Legende zu den einzelnen Positionen (in verschiedenen Benennungen): 1 Feuerboden, Kaminboden, Herdboden; 2 Rost, Aschenrost; 3 Feueröffnung, Kaminöffnung, Strahlungsöffnung, Heizöffnung, Kaminloch, Feuerloch, Herdloch; 4 Feuerraum, Herdraum, Feuerstelle, Herd; 5 Feuerraumseitenwand; 6 Feuerraumrückwand, Herdwand; 7 Rauchhals; 8 Rauchkehle; 9 Rauchklappe, Drosselklappe, Regulierklappe, Zugklappe; 10 Rauchsims, Rauchmulde, Umkehrboden, Umlenkboden; 11 Rauchkammer, Rauchsammler; 12 Schornstein, Rauchrohr, Rauchkanal, Rauchabzug; 13 Rauchschürze, Rauchklappe, Rauchschild, Rauchmantel, Rauchglocke, Rauchhaube, ebenso Kaminschürze, Kamin... usw.; 14 Zuluftkanal, Frischluftkanal, Luftkanal; 15 Sicherheitsstreifen, Vorplatte, Funkenschutzstreifen; 16 Aschenfall, Aschenkanal, Aschenschacht; 17 Aschenkammer, Aschengrube, Aschenhöhle; 18 Putztür, Reinigungstür.

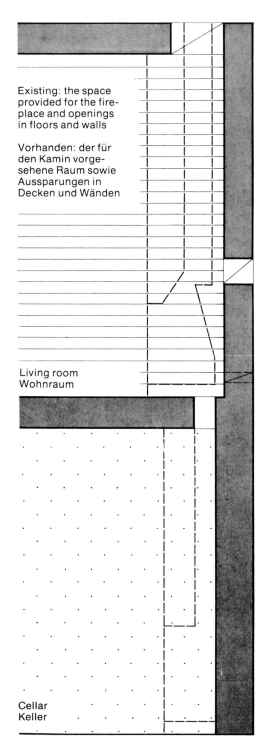

Existing: the space
provided for the fire-
place and openings
in floors and walls

Vorhanden: der für
den Kamin vorge-
sehene Raum sowie
Aussparungen in
Decken und Wänden

Living room
Wohnraum

Cellar
Keller

## Constructional guides

The following sections deal with the structural components of the open fireplace. A reliable and widely-used type, which may be termed as a "standard fireplace" serves as demonstration example. Its inner structure and proportions constitute, in modified or simplified form, the technical principles for many other fireplace solutions. The following guides have been compiled from the standpoint of maximal performance and perfect functioning. Should they, however, be less rigidly observed in practice, a substantial forfeit in performance need not necessarily follow. In fireplace construction, as in many other technical branches, the most irregular solutions have often led to acceptable results, but the risk of course is correspondingly high.

Now and again, the opinion is even voiced that the heating performance of a fireplace is insignificant, since as a rule another heating system takes over the actual heating function of the room. Without doubt the view that the fireplace is a purely decorative element, a type of painting with movable content, is very questionable. The results of years of research work, undertaken by experts and experienced industrial enterprises, clearly demonstrate that the range of utilization of the fireplace is much wider and its functional value much higher than generally assumed.

The design pattern for the construction of open fireplaces shows the sequence for determining the individual items, both in modern houses as well as old houses. The corresponding dimensions may by found in the table of measurements on page 16.

*Fireplace construction in modern houses*
a) Ascertain the given or desired room size in $m^3$.
b) Locate the value which approximately corresponds with the room size ascertained under a) in the table, under R. Determine the required size of the fireplace opening from the same horizontal column, under FF = A x B.
c) Establish the chimney cross-section according to the table, under J and K, taking the total height of the chimney, from centre firebox to top edge chimney top, into consideration (see note on chimney heights in the table on page 16).
d) Determine the dimensions of the firebox according to A, B, C + 5–10 cm and D, the throat according to F, G and H.
e) The dimensions of the remaining items, such as smoke shelf and smoke chamber become apparent from the drawing or may be looked up under the individual key words.

*Fireplace construction in old houses*
a) An open fireplace may be subsequently installed in any appropriate room, provided the static overload arising from the weight of the fireplace can be accommodated, and the chimney can be guided without too much difficulty. After determining the size of the room, the construction of the fireplace is carried out on the same principles as in modern buildings.

b) If a useable chimney connection already exists, it is important to check whether the chimney for the proposed fireplace has any additional connections; these must be closed off and all joints must be sealed.
c) Compare measurements of chimney cross-section and room size ascertained under a) with the corresponding values in the table.
d) If the values determined under a) approximately coincide with the table values, the dimensions of fireplace items may be determined according to the table.
e) If the relationship between room size and chimney cross-section does not correspond with the table values (slight deviations may be disregarded), the decision must be made to either accept the inevitable laborious and expensive alterations or do without the fireplace altogether.
f) It may be possible, in very large rooms, to draw a partitioning wall, so that the new room area approximately corresponds with the table values i. e. with the existing chimney cross-section.
g) In normal-sized rooms, only the chimney cross-section may be altered. If this is too excessive, the cross-section may be reduced to the required measurement by casing the chimney with hard-burned clay pipes. It is however better to erect a new chimney.
h) If the chimney cross-section is too small, the erection of a new chimney is the only possible solution.
i) If one of the measures suggested under f)–h) has been carried out, and the resulting measurements coincide with the table values, the dimensions of the remaining items may be determined according to the usual procedure.

1. Wall-incorporated fireplaces constitute a major element of the house structure and are unsuitable for subsequent installation. (Hale Matthews Residence, East Hampton, New York, designed by Alfredo De Vido.)
2. Freestanding fireplaces, on the other hand, are suitably adapted for subsequent installation as well. (House in Histon near Cambridge, England, designed by David Thurlow.)
3. The simplest solution is the connection to an existing chimney by means of pipe junctions. (House in Brabrand, Denmark, designed by Nils Primdahl & Erich Weitling.)

## Konstruktionshinweise

Die folgenden Abschnitte behandeln die konstruktiven Bestandteile des offenen Kamins. Als Anschauungsbeispiel dient ein bewährter und weitverbreiteter Typ, den man als „Standardkamin" bezeichnen könnte. Seine Innenkonstruktion und seine Maßverhältnisse bilden in abgewandelter oder vereinfachter Form die technische Grundlage für viele andere Kaminlösungen. Die hier folgenden Hinweise sind unter dem Gesichtspunkt maximaler Leistung und einwandfreier Funktion zusammengestellt. Werden sie in der Praxis weniger streng befolgt, so muß das nicht unbedingt eine wesentliche Leistungseinbuße zur Folge haben. Wie auf manchem anderen technischen Gebiet gibt es auch beim Kaminbau Fälle, in denen die regelwidrigsten Lösungen zu annehmbaren Ergebnissen führen, allerdings ist das Risiko entsprechend hoch.

Manchmal begegnet man sogar der Meinung, die Wärmeleistung eines Kamins sei unwesentlich, da in der Regel ja doch ein anderes Heizsystem die eigentliche Raumerwärmung übernähme. Die Fragwürdigkeit dieser Auffassung, die im Kamin nur noch ein rein dekoratives Element, eine Art Bild mit beweglichem Inhalt sieht, steht außer Zweifel. Hält man ihr die Ergebnisse jahrelanger Forschungsarbeiten von Experten und erfahrenen Industrieunternehmen entgegen, so demonstrieren diese eindeutig, daß der Anwendungsbereich des Kamins weitaus vielseitiger und sein Nutzwert wesentlich höher ist, als allgemein angenommen wird.

Das Entwurfsschema für die Konstruktion offener Kamine zeigt die Reihenfolge für die Festlegung der einzelnen Positionen, und zwar bei Neubauten und bei Altbauten. Die entsprechenden Maßwerte sind der Bemessungstabelle auf Seite 16 zu entnehmen.

*Kaminkonstruktion in Neubauten*
a) Die gegebene oder gewünschte Raumgröße in m³ ermitteln.
b) In der Tabelle unter R den Wert aufsuchen, der ungefähr der unter a) ermittelten Raumgröße entspricht. Bestimmen der erforderlichen Feueröffnungsgröße aus der gleichen waagrechten Spalte unter FF = A x B.
c) Festlegen des Schornsteinquerschnitts nach der Tabelle unter J und K, unter Berücksichtigung der gesamten Schornsteinhöhe, gemessen von Mitte Feuerraum bis Oberkante Schornsteinkopf (siehe Anmerkung über Schornsteinhöhen zu der Tabelle auf Seite 16).
d) Dimensionieren des Feuerraums nach A, B, C + 5–10 cm und D, des Rauchhalses nach F, G und H.
e) Die Abmessungen der übrigen Positionen wie Rauchsims und Rauchkammer ergeben sich beim Aufzeichnen oder können unter den einzelnen Stichworten nachgeschlagen werden.

*Kaminkonstruktion in Altbauten*
a) Ein offener Kamin läßt sich auch nachträglich in jedem geeigneten Raum einbauen, vorausgesetzt, daß die durch das Kamingewicht auftretende statische Mehrbelastung aufgenommen werden kann und die Führung des Schornsteins keine allzu große Schwierigkeiten bereitet. Nach Ermittlung der Größe des vorhandenen Raums verfährt man wie bei Kaminkonstruktionen in Neubauten.
b) Existiert ein benutzbarer Schornsteinanschluß, so muß festgestellt werden, ob noch andere Anschlüsse an dem für den Kamin vorgesehenen Schornstein vorhanden sind; diese sind stillzulegen und fugendicht zu verschließen.
c) Vergleichen der unter a) ermittelten Maße von Schornsteinquerschnitt und Raumgröße mit den entsprechenden Werten in der Tabelle.
d) Decken sich die unter a) erhaltenen Werte annähernd mit den Tabellenwerten, so können die Kaminpositionen nach der Tabelle dimensioniert werden.
e) Sollte das Verhältnis von Raumgröße und Schornsteinquerschnitt nicht den Tabellenwerten entsprechen (kleine Abweichungen können selbstverständlich außer Betracht bleiben), so muß entschieden werden, ob es besser ist, umständliche und kostspielige Umbauarbeiten auf sich zu nehmen oder ganz auf den Kamin zu verzichten.
f) Bei sehr großen Räumen läßt sich unter Umständen eine Zwischenwand einziehen, so daß die neue Raumfläche ungefähr den Tabellenwerten beziehungsweise dem vorhandenen Schornsteinquerschnitt entspricht.
g) In Räumen von normaler Größe kann nur der Schornsteinquerschnitt verändert werden. Ist dieser zu groß, so besteht die Möglichkeit, den Querschnitt durch Auffüttern mit hartgebrannten Tonrohren auf das erforderliche Maß zu reduzieren. Besser ist jedoch auf jeden Fall die Erstellung eines neuen Schornsteins.
h) Bei zu kleinem Schornsteinquerschnitt bleibt nur der Weg, einen neuen Schornstein zu errichten.
i) Wurde eine der unter f) – h) genannten Maßnahmen durchgeführt und stimmen die erhaltenen Maße mit den Tabellenwerten überein, so wird die Dimensionierung der übrigen Positionen nach dem üblichen Verfahren vorgenommen.

1

2

3

1. Wandbündige Kamine bilden einen festen Bestandteil im Gefüge des Hauses und eignen sich schlecht zum nachträglichen Einbau. (Hale Matthews Residence, East Hampton, New York, entworfen von Alfredo De Vido.)
2. Frei stehende Kamine sind dagegen auch für den nachträglichen Einbau geeignet. (Haus in Histon bei Cambridge, England, entworfen von David Thurlow.)
3. Die einfachste Lösung ist der Anschluß an einen vorhandenen Schornstein mittels Rohrstutzen. (Haus in Brabrand, Dänemark, entworfen von Nils Primdahl & Erich Weitling.)

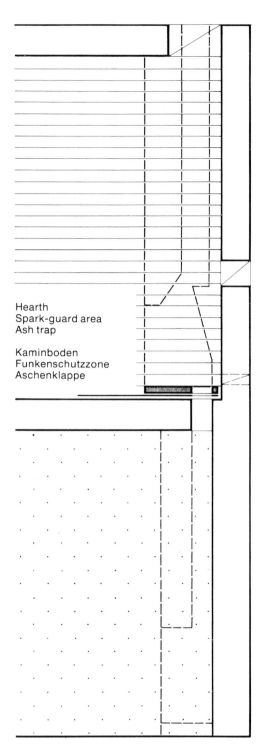

Hearth
Spark-guard area
Ash trap

Kaminboden
Funkenschutzzone
Aschenklappe

## Hearth/Safety

The hearth, which forms the bottom surface of the firebox, must be composed of refractory material (in massive constructions, minimal thickness for solid bricks 11,5 cm, for concrete 10 cm; minimal thickness of lining material such as firebricks or clinker bricks 6 cm). Additional insulation under the hearth is advisable, in timber-joist floors indispensable. Fireclay, asbestos, kieselguhr, sheets of glass wool or mineral wool are considered suitable insulating materials. An additional air gap between the hearth and the floor is the safest method of insulation.

There are three possible locations for the hearth: firstly, sunken below the room floor (a seldom solution, satisfactory functioning depends on fresh-air supply through floor or wall ducts, a favourable, natural recess for embers and ash); Secondly, level with the room floor (required minimum height of fireplace opening, as with the sunken hearth, about 70 cm, otherwise flames are not completely visible and heat radiation is unsatisfactory, hearth and safety area may be combined as single area); thirdly, raised above the level of the room floor (good view of flames, favourable heat radiation, simple to operate, also suitable for smaller fireplace openings).

Statutory regulations, and, it these do not exist, the general rules laid down by the fire prevention authority specify certain structural safety measures for the construction of a fireplace; they require that the fireplace have a fireproof underlayer and that all parts connected to it be safeguarded against ignition through heat or flying sparks. The room floor must be protected against flying sparks by a safety area of refractory material (solid bricks, slabs, concrete, metal plate with asbestos underlayer etc.), which must have a depth of at least 15–20 cm on either side. If the hearth lies higher than 30 cm above the room floor, further safety measures will be necessary (see figs. 25–27 and section "Fireplace opening"). Apart from fireproofing, the following must be considered: dampproofing as protection against condensation (in fireplaces in exterior walls) as well as rising ground moisture (in fireplaces with own fundament), and heat insulation to prevent excessive heat loss.

## Kaminboden/Sicherheit

Der Kaminboden, der die untere Begrenzung des Feuerraums bildet, muß aus feuerbeständigem Material bestehen (bei Massivkonstruktionen Mindeststärke für Vollsteine 11,5 cm, für Beton 10 cm; Mindeststärke des Auskleidungsmaterials wie Schamotte- oder Klinkersteine 6 cm). Eine zusätzliche Isolierung unter dem Kaminboden ist ratsam, bei Holzbalkendecken sogar unerläßlich. Als Isoliermaterial kommen Schamotte, Asbest, Kieselgur, Glas- oder Mineralwolleplatten in Betracht. Am sichersten isoliert ein zusätzlicher Luftraum zwischen Kaminboden und Decke.

Für die Lage des Kaminbodens gibt es drei Möglichkeiten: erstens unter dem Niveau des Zimmerbodens (selten vorkommend, gute Funktion abhängig von Frischluftzufuhr durch Boden- oder Wandkanäle, günstige, natürliche Mulde für Glut und Asche); zweitens bündig mit dem Zimmerboden (erforderliche Mindesthöhe der Feueröffnung wie bei tieferliegendem Kaminboden etwa 70 cm, da sonst Flammenbild nicht voll sichtbar und Wärmestrahlung ungünstig, Kaminboden und Sicherheitsstreifen zu einheitlicher Fläche zusammenfaßbar); drittens über dem Niveau des Zimmerbodens (gut sichtbares Flammenbild, günstige Wärmestrahlung, einfache Bedienung, auch kleinere Feueröffnungen verwendbar).

Gesetzliche Vorschriften und, wo diese fehlen, die allgemeinen Richtlinien der Feuerschutzbehörden schreiben für die Konstruktion eines Kamins bestimmte bauliche Sicherheitsmaßnahmen vor; so verlangen sie eine feuersichere Unterlage und die Absicherung aller an den Kamin anschließenden Bauteile gegen Entzündung durch Hitze oder Funkenflug. Der Zimmerboden muß vor Funkenflug durch einen Sicherheitsstreifen aus feuerbeständigem Material (Vollsteine, Platten, Beton, Metallblech mit Asbestunterlage usw.) geschützt werden, der mindestens eine Tiefe von 50 cm und einen seitlichen Überstand von 15–20 cm haben sollte. Liegt der Feuerboden höher als 30 cm über dem Zimmerboden, so werden zusätzliche Sicherungsmaßnahmen erforderlich (vgl. Abb. 25–27 und Abschnitt „Feueröffnung"). Neben der Feuerschutzisolierung sind zu beachten: die Feuchtigkeitsisolierung als Schutz gegen Tauwasserbildung (bei Kaminen in Außenwänden) und aufsteigende Bodenfeuchtigkeit (bei Kaminen mit eigenem Fundament) und die Wärmeisolierung, die einen übermäßigen Wärmeverlust vermeiden soll.

1–12. Various locations of the hearth for fireplaces with one-sided (figs. 1–6) and multi-sided fireplace openings (figs. 7–12). (Figs. 1, 7: hearth level with the floor; figs. 2, 8: sunken hearth; figs. 3, 9: sunken hearth, fire grate level with the floor; figs. 4, 10: raised hearth; figs. 5, 11: hearth level with the floor, fire grate raised; figs. 6, 12: raised hearth on wood-beam floor, with air space between floor and hearth.)
13–18. Various types of fire bed. (Figs. 13, 14: firedogs of clinker or firebricks; fig. 15: prefabricated firebridge of fireclay from the company

Cheminée Honegger, Zurich; fig. 16: iron grate lying on flat-iron bars embedded in concrete; fig. 17: iron grate of four-cornered iron bars, supported on an underframe; fig. 18: andirons of four-cornered iron.)
19–24. Safety areas of various types of fireplace. (Fig. 19: freestanding fireplace; fig. 20: fireplace at a wall projection; fig. 21: corner fireplace at an open angle; fig. 22: corner fireplace at a projecting room corner; fig. 23: wall-incorporated fireplace; fig. 24: fireplace hanging in front of a wall.)

25–27. Safety area of elevated hearth. The longer flight parabola of the sparks may be shortened by the following measures: placing a fine-meshed screen in front of the fireplace opening (fig. 25); fitting a fine-meshed screen, at least 15 cm in height, into the fireplace opening (fig. 26); raising the safety area to hearth level, thus adapting to the minimum measurements of a level-with-the-floor solution.

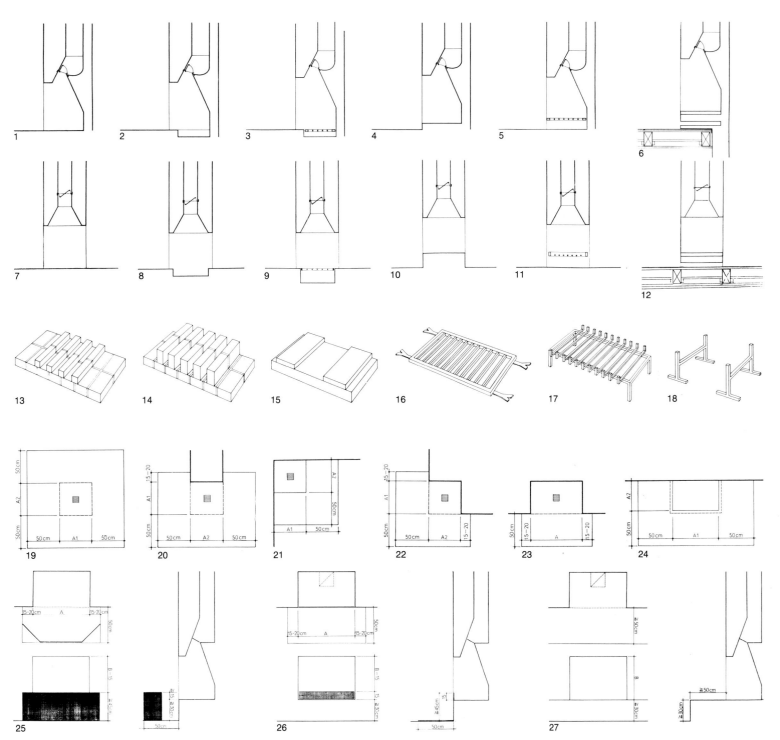

1–12. Verschiedene Ausführungen des Kaminbodens für Kamine mit einseitiger (Abb. 1–6) und mehrseitiger Feueröffnung (Abb. 7–12). (Abb. 1, 7: fußbodengleicher Kaminboden; Abb. 2, 8: vertiefter Kaminboden; Abb. 3, 9: vertiefter Kaminboden, Feuerrost fußbodengleich; Abb. 4, 10: erhöhter Kaminboden; Abb. 5, 11: Kaminboden fußbodengleich, Rost erhöht; Abb. 6, 12: erhöhter Kaminboden auf Holzbalkendecke mit Luftraum zwischen Decke und Kaminboden.)

13–18. Verschiedene Ausführungen des Feuerbodens. (Abb. 13, 14: Feuerböcke aus Klinkern oder Schamottesteinen; Abb. 15: vorgefertigter Feuerbock aus Schamotte der Firma Cheminée Honegger, Zürich; Abb. 16: Eisenrost, auf einbetoniertem Flacheisen aufliegend; Abb. 17: Eisenrost aus Vierkanteisen auf Untergestell; Abb. 18: Kaminböcke aus Vierkanteisen.)

19–24. Sicherheitsstreifen bei verschiedenen Kaminarten. (Abb. 19: frei stehender Kamin; Abb. 20: Kamin an Mauerzunge; Abb. 21: Eckkamin in offenem Winkel; Abb. 22: Eckkamin in vorspringender Raumecke; Abb. 23: wandbündiger Kamin; Abb. 24: vorgehängter Kamin.)

25–27. Sicherheitsstreifen bei hochliegendem Feuerboden. Die größere Flugparabel der Funken kann durch folgende Maßnahmen verkürzt werden: Aufstellung eines engmaschigen Gitterschirms vor der Feueröffnung (Abb. 25); Anbringung eines engmaschigen Gitterschirms von mindestens 15 cm Höhe in der Feueröffnung (Abb. 26); Anhebung des Sicherheitsbereichs auf Feuerbodenniveau, dadurch Angleichung an die Mindestmaße einer fußbodengleichen Lösung (Abb. 27).

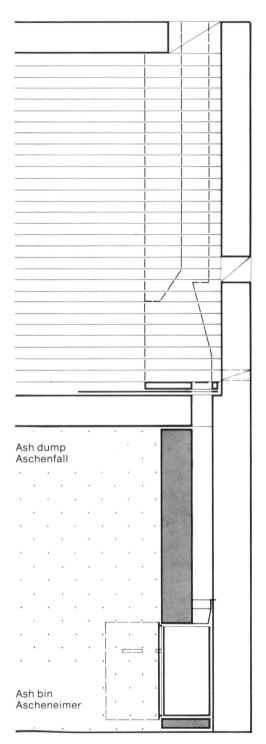

Ash dump
Aschenfall

Ash bin
Ascheneimer

## Devices for ash removal

The time-consuming and dirty task of removing the ash from the hearth may be facilitated by the installation of an ash-removal device. The most widely-used solution are:

a) Ash box of iron plate with hinged pouring-grate. The box is mounted into the hearth in such a way that the top edge is flush with the hearth. It is removed by means of a handle.

b) Ash tub of iron plate with hinged pouring-grate and two handles for easy removal. The ash tub is especially suitable for sunken hearths.

c) Ash drawer of iron plate with mounting frame and guide rail, which may be built into the base of the fireplace or hung beneath the floor. A lid or grate is fitted into the hearth.

d) Ash bin of galvanized steel plate with short feed pipe in the lid, located on the lower floor. A galvanized pipeline leads to a connecting pipe which is embedded in the floor and opens out into the hearth. It is covered with a lid or a grate in the hearth (advantage: the bin has a greater holding capacity, the ash need not be carried out through the room). If the fireplace is situated at an exterior wall, the ash bin may even be fitted outside of the house. It is essential to examine the bin lid and pipeline for leaks, at regular intervals, since the latter will result in the infiltration of false air.

e) Ash dump and ash pit on the lower floor, which may also be solid constructions of brick or concrete. Similarly, the chimney may be extended accordingly to the basement area, in which case it is necessary to ensure that smoke flue and ash dump are separated by means of an airtight locking device.

## Aschenfallkonstruktionen

Die zeitraubende und schmutzige Beseitigung der Asche vom Kaminboden läßt sich durch den Einbau einer Aschenfalleinrichtung erleichtern. Die bekanntesten Lösungen sind:

a) Aschenbehälter aus Eisenblech mit aufklappbarem Gußrost. Der Behälter wird so in den Kaminboden eingelassen, daß er oben bündig abschließt. Zum Entleeren kann man ihn mittels eines Handgriffs herausnehmen.

b) Aschenwanne aus Eisenblech mit aufklappbarem Gußrost und zwei Handgriffen zum Herausnehmen. Die Wanne ist besonders geeignet bei muldenartiger Vertiefung des Kaminbodens.

c) Aschenschublade aus Eisenblech mit Einbaurahmen und Laufschiene, zum Einbau in den Kaminsockel oder unter der Geschoßdecke hängend. In den Kaminboden wird ein Abfalldeckel oder ein Rost eingesetzt.

d) Ascheneimer aus verzinktem Eisenblech im Untergeschoß, mit Stutzen im Deckel. Eine verzinkte Rohrleitung führt zu einem Anschlußrohr, das in die Decke einbetoniert wird und in den Kaminboden mündet. Die Abdeckung erfolgt durch einen Aschenfalldeckel oder einen Rost im Kaminboden (Vorteil: größeres Fassungsvermögen des Eimers, kein Aschentransport durchs Zimmer). Ist der Kamin an einer Außenwand plaziert, so kann der Aschenbehälter sogar außerhalb des Hauses angebracht werden. In gewissen Zeitabständen ist allerdings zu prüfen, ob Eimerdeckel und Rohrleitung noch dicht sind, da sonst Falschluftzuführung auftritt.

e) Aschenfallschacht und Aschenkammer im Untergeschoß können auch massiv aus Ziegeln oder Beton hergestellt werden. Ebenso läßt sich die Verlängerung des Schornsteins in den Kellerbereich entsprechend ausbauen, wobei jedoch zu beachten ist, daß Rauchrohr und Aschenfallschacht durch eine luftdichte Sperrvorrichtung voneinander getrennt werden.

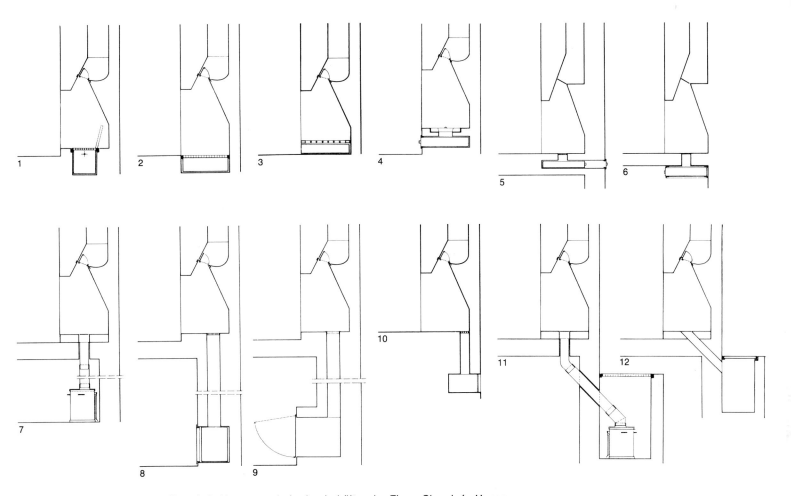

1. Ash box from the company Cheminée Honegger, Zurich. Emptied from the room.
2. Ash tub. Emptied from the room.
3. Ash drawer arranged under the fire grate. Emptied from the room.
4. Ash drawer from the company Cheminée Honegger, Zurich. Emptied from the room.
5. Ash drawer in a ceiling recess. Emptied from the exterior.
6. Ash drawer hanging beneath the floor. Emptied from the lower floor.
7. Ash-removal device from the company Cheminée Honegger, Zurich, with ash bin in the basement. Emptied in the basement.
8. Ash-removal device with ash bin in a wall niche in the basement and solid ash dump.
9. Solid ash-removal device with ash pit in the basement. Emptied from the basement.
10. Solid ash-removal device with ash pit in the basement. Emptied from the exterior.
11. Ash-removal device with ash bin in an external dump. Emptied out of doors.
12. Solid ash-removal device with ash pit outside. Emptied out of doors.

1. Aschenbehälter der Firma Cheminée Honegger, Zürich. Entleerung vom Zimmer her.
2. Aschenwanne. Entleerung vom Zimmer her.
3. Aschenschublade, unter dem Feuerrost angeordnet. Entleerung vom Zimmer her.
4. Aschenschublade der Firma Cheminée Honegger, Zürich. Entleerung vom Zimmer her.
5. Aschenschublade in Deckenaussparung. Entleerung von außen.
6. Aschenschublade unter der Geschoßdecke hängend. Entleerung vom Untergeschoß aus.
7. Aschenfallkonstruktion der Firma Cheminée Honegger, Zürich, mit Ascheneimer im Keller. Entleerung im Keller.
8. Aschenfallkonstruktion mit Ascheneimer im Keller in einer Mauernische und massivem Aschenfallkanal.
9. Massive Aschenfallkonstruktion mit Aschenkammer im Keller. Entleerung vom Keller her.
10. Massive Aschenfallkonstruktion mit Aschenkammer im Keller. Entleerung von außen.
11. Aschenfallkonstruktion mit Ascheneimer in einem Außenschacht. Entleerung im Freien.
12. Massive Aschenfallkonstruktion mit Aschenkammer im Freien. Entleerung im Freien.

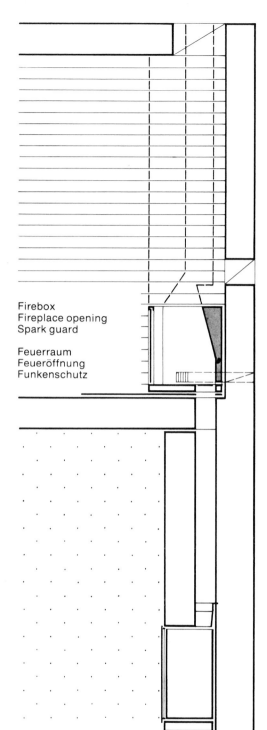

Firebox
Fireplace opening
Spark guard

Feuerraum
Feueröffnung
Funkenschutz

## Fireplace opening/Firebox

Radiation of warmth and visibility of flames depend largely upon the size and location of the fireplace opening. The opening should ideally be wider than high, since a rectangle has proved to be the most suitable shape. A low opening creates a better draught than a high one; nevertheless, the height should be so proportioned that a good view is afforded into the fireplace opening (approximate measurement: 70 cm from room floor to top edge fireplace opening). Height and width are determined by the cubic capacity of the room to be heated and by the chimney cross-section. Simple tables are available today to facilitate the determination of the dimensions. The proportions may be roughly estimated according to the following rules of thumb:
a) Chimney cross-sectional area = 10% of the area of the fireplace opening, by an average chimney height of about 10 m (tolerance 6–12 m).
b) The height B of the fireplace opening, in normal-sized rooms, is about $3/4$ of width A, in very large rooms on the other hand, $2/3$ of width A.
c) The proportion of the fireplace-opening area: room area is 1:40 to 1:70.
The figures 4–8 show various safety grates and curtains which may be fitted in front of the fireplace opening as protection against flying sparks. Metal blinds or sliding plate screens increase the draught by reducing the cross-section of the opening, thus facilitating the lighting of the fire; in addition, they help to regulate the consumption of the fire and close the opening when the fireplace is not in use.
The firebox is the nucleus of a fireplace; its perfect functioning presupposes correct dimensioning. Hereby, it is essential to adhere to specific proportions between the height B, the width A and the depth C as stipulated in the table on page 16. A comparison shows that the depth of the firebox is approximately $1/2$ the width of the opening A or $2/3$ the height of the opening B. Normally, it is not less than 45 cm (otherwise smoke diffusion results), in larger fireplaces not more than 60 cm (otherwise high loss of radiant heat results). Slight skewing of the side walls (about 20°) and forward tilting of the back wall of 10–20 cm, from about $1/3$ height of the opening to the fireplace opening (see the drawing on page 17), increases the radiation of heat; for reasons of form, however, vertical walls are often preferred.

## Feueröffnung/Feuerraum

Wärmestrahlung und Sichtbarkeit des Flammenbildes hängen weitgehend von Größe und Lage der Feueröffnung ab. Am günstigsten erwies sich die Form eines liegenden Rechtecks. Eine niedrige Öffnung schafft bessere Zugverhältnisse als eine hohe, doch sollte die Höhe so bemessen sein, daß man gut in die Feueröffnung hineinsehen kann (Annäherungswert: 70 cm vom Zimmerboden bis Oberkante Feueröffnung). Ihre Höhe und Breite wird durch den Kubikinhalt des zu beheizenden Raumes und durch den Schornsteinquerschnitt bestimmt. Die Abmessungen lassen sich heute leicht mit Hilfe einfacher Tabellen ermitteln. Für eine überschlägige Bemessung ist mit folgenden Faustregeln auszukommen:
a) Schornsteinquerschnittsfläche = 10 % der Fläche der Feueröffnung bei einer mittleren Schornsteinhöhe von etwa 10 m (Toleranz 6–12 m).
b) Die Höhe B der Feueröffnung beträgt bei Räumen mit den üblichen Abmessungen ungefähr $3/4$ der Breite A, bei sehr großen Räumen dagegen $2/3$ der Breite A.
c) Die Feueröffnungsfläche steht im Verhältnis 1:40 bis 1:70 zur Raumfläche.
Die Abbildungen 4–8 zeigen verschiedene Sicherheitsgitter und -vorhänge, die zur Vermeidung von Funkenflug vor der Feueröffnung angebracht werden können. Metalljalousien oder verstellbare Blechschirme verstärken bei Verkleinerung des Öffnungsquerschnitts den Zug und erleichtern dadurch das Anheizen; außerdem bewirken sie eine begrenzte Regulierung des Abbrandes und verschließen die Kaminöffnung bei Nichtbenutzung.
Der Feuerraum bildet das Kernstück einer Kaminanlage, seine richtige Dimensionierung ist Voraussetzung für ein einwandfreies Funktionieren. Dabei sind, wie der Tabelle auf Seite 16 zu entnehmen ist, bestimmte Verhältnisse zwischen der Höhe B, der Breite A und der Tiefe C einzuhalten. Ein Vergleich zeigt, daß die Tiefe des Feuerraums ungefähr $1/2$ der Öffnungsbreite A oder $2/3$ der Öffnungshöhe B ausmacht. Normalerweise liegt sie nicht unter 45 cm (sonst Rauchausschlag), bei größeren Kaminen nicht über 60 cm (sonst hoher Verlust an Strahlungswärme). Leichtes Schrägstellen der Seitenwände (etwa um 20°) und Vorneigen der Rückwand ungefähr ab $1/3$ der Öffnungshöhe um 10–20 cm zur Feueröffnung hin (vgl. die Zeichnung auf Seite 17) erhöht die Wärmeausstrahlung; aus formalen Gründen werden aber vielfach gerade Wände bevorzugt.

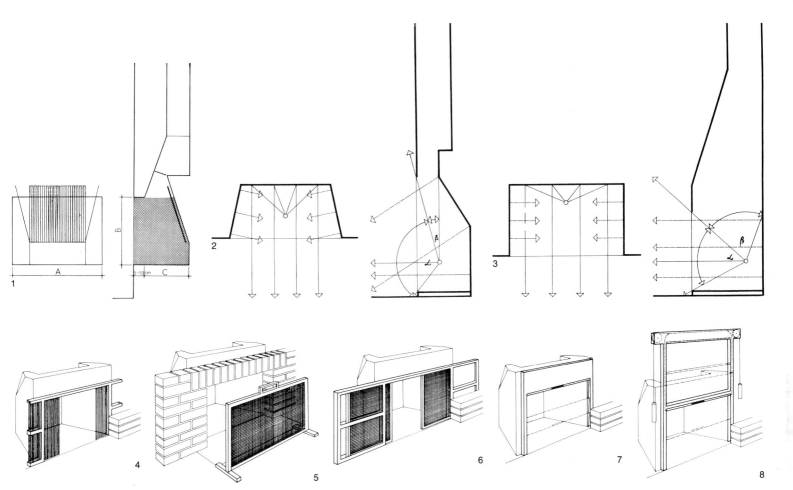

1. Normal fireplace; a ribbed cast-iron plate on the sloping firebox back wall increases the radiation intensity.

2. Modern fireplace construction with small firebox depth, smoke shelf, forward-sloping back wall and skewing side walls. In comparison with example 3, the functional diagram shows a considerable increase in the useful radiation power (angle $\alpha$ = useful radiation, $\beta$ = radiation loss) as the result of optimal shaping of the fireplace interior according to principles of radiation and aerodynamics (according to W. Häusler).

3. Fireplace with large firebox depth, without smoke shelf, with straight back wall, parallel side walls; correspondingly low useful radiation, high radiation loss (according to W. Häusler).

4–8. Additional safety and closing devices for the fireplace opening. (Fig. 4: spark curtain of metallic texture with mounting frame, from the company Cheminée Honegger, Zurich; fig. 5: fireguard mounted on a frame; fig. 6: sliding doors of metallic texture with mounting frame; fig. 7: three-piece jalousie from the company Cheminée Honegger, Zurich; fig. 8: draw-plate running on counterweights, infinitely adjustable.)

1. Normalkamin; eine gerippte Gußplatte an der geneigten Feuerraumrückwand erhöht die Strahlungsintensität.

2. Kamin moderner Bauart mit kleiner Feuerraumtiefe, Rauchsims, geneigter Rückwand und schräggestellten Seitenwänden. Im Vergleich mit Beispiel 3 zeigt das Funktionsbild eine beträchtliche Erhöhung des Nutzstrahlungseffekts (Winkel $\alpha$ = Nutzstrahlung, $\beta$ = Verluststrahlung) als Ergebnis einer optimalen Ausformung des Kamininnern nach strahlungs- und strömungstechnischen Gesichtspunkten (nach W. Häusler).

3. Kamin mit großer Feuerraumtiefe, ohne Rauchsims, mit gerader Rückwand, parallelgestellten Seitenwänden; entsprechend geringere Nutzstrahlung, hoher Strahlungsverlust (nach W. Häusler).

4–8. Zusätzliche Sicherheits- und Verschlußvorrichtung für die Feueröffnung. (Abb. 4: Kaminvorhang aus Metallgewebe mit Einbaurahmen der Firma Cheminée Honegger, Zürich; Abb. 5: Vorstellgitter, in Rahmen gefaßt; Abb. 6: Schiebetüren aus Metallgewebe mit Einbaurahmen; Abb. 7: dreiteilige Kaminjalousie der Firma Cheminée Honegger, Zürich; Abb. 8: Zugschild, an Gegengewichten laufend, stufenlos verstellbar.)

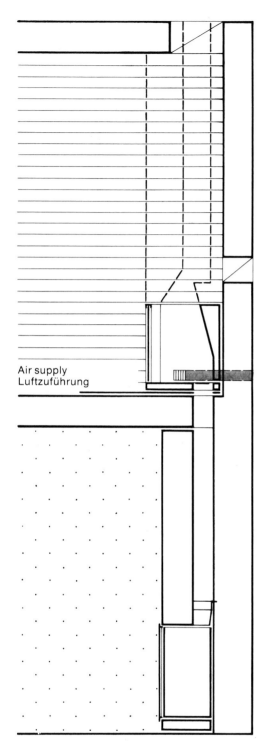

Air supply
Luftzuführung

## Air supply

One of the most important conditions for the combustion of the fire, is the adequate and unimpaired supply of fresh air, which need not necessarily come directly from the out of doors. In many cases it is withdrawn from the room (room air). This of course presupposes a constant inflow of air to the room, for which leaks in windows and doors often provide adequately. If however the fire has excessive updraught, there is a danger of unpleasant draught within the room. For this reason, the trend to provide an air supply independent of the room has become manifest in recent years. There are three basic methods of supplying the fire with fresh air:
a) One makes use of the air inflow through leaks in windows and doors (fig. 8). Tightly closing doors may of course also be planed down or an air vent may be cut into them (fig. 9).
b) The ash removal device may be fitted with air vents or connected to air ducts (figs. 1–4).
c) The ideal solution, however, is the direct supply of outside air to the fire area by means of air ducts, which either run in or under the floor or lead directly to the exterior in the form of wall ducts (figs. 5, 6). Hereby, it is essential to introduce the air at the lowest possible point, but without whirling up the ash in the process. For this reason alone, it is advisable to separate hearth and ash bed (e. g. with a firedog). The air-duct outlets in the hearth should be covered over with a screen, the external suction opening must be fitted with a shutter. The air ducts can be used as an additional means of room ventilation when the fire is not in use.

## Luftzuführung

Eine der wichtigsten Voraussetzungen für den Abbrand des Feuers ist die ausreichende und störungsfreie Zufuhr frischer Luft, die jedoch nicht unbedingt aus dem Freien kommen muß. In vielen Fällen wird sie aus dem Zimmer angesaugt (Raumluft). Das ist natürlich nur dann möglich, wenn genügend Luft in das Zimmer nachströmen kann, wofür oft schon undichte Fenster und Türen ausreichen. Bei zu starkem Zug des Kamins besteht dabei allerdings die Gefahr unangenehmer Zugerscheinungen im Raum. Deshalb setzt sich gerade in den letzten Jahren die raumunabhängige Luftzuführung immer mehr durch. Es gibt drei grundsätzliche Möglichkeiten, dem Kaminfeuer Frischluft zuzuführen:
a) Man nutzt die Undichtigkeit von Fenstern und Türen aus (Abb. 8). Natürlich kann man auch dicht schließende Türen abhobeln oder einen Lüftungsschlitz ausschneiden (Abb. 9).
b) Die Aschenfallkonstruktion wird mit Luftschlitzen versehen oder mit Luftkanälen verbunden (Abb. 1–4).
c) Die beste Lösung ist jedoch die direkte Frischluftzuführung von außen in die Feuerstelle, und zwar durch Zuluftkanäle, die entweder in bzw. unter der Decke verlaufen oder als Wandkanal unmittelbar ins Freie führen (Abb. 5, 6). Dabei ist es wichtig, die Luftzuführung so tief wie möglich anzusetzen, doch ohne daß dabei die Asche aufgewirbelt würde. Schon aus diesem Grund ist es besser, Feuer- und Aschenboden zu trennen (etwa durch einen Feuerbock). Die Luftaustrittsöffnung in der Feuerstelle sollte mit einem Gitter abgedeckt werden, die äußere Ansaugöffnung muß mit einer Klappe verschließbar sein. Die Luftkanäle können zusätzlich zur Raumbelüftung verwendet werden, wenn das Feuer nicht brennt.

1–9. Various methods of supplying the fire with air. (Fig. 1: air supply from the basement via the ash dump; fig. 2: air supply through a vent in the ash drawer; fig. 3: air supply through a vent in the base; fig. 4: air supply from the exterior via the ash dump; fig. 5: air duct in the fireplace wall leading directly to the exterior; fig. 6: air duct hanging beneath the floor, leading to the exterior; fig. 7: air duct leading to the basement, air drawn from the lower floor area; fig. 8: the normal movement tolerance of a door is often sufficient for an adequate air supply; fig. 9: it is

better to cut out air vents or holes in the bottom part of the door.)
10–13. Examples showing how air is supplied with the fireplace unit "Superfire" from the company Kaminbau Burgers Söhne, Thörishaus/Bern. (Fig. 10: the supply air is collected directly under the fireplace; fig. 11: if the fireplace is situated at an exterior wall, the fresh air may be conveyed directly form the exterior to the back of the fireplace; fig. 12: if the fresh air is collected in the attic or over the roof, it is supplied to the fire through a duct which runs

parallel to the chimney; fig. 13: flow of air currents and combustion gases.)

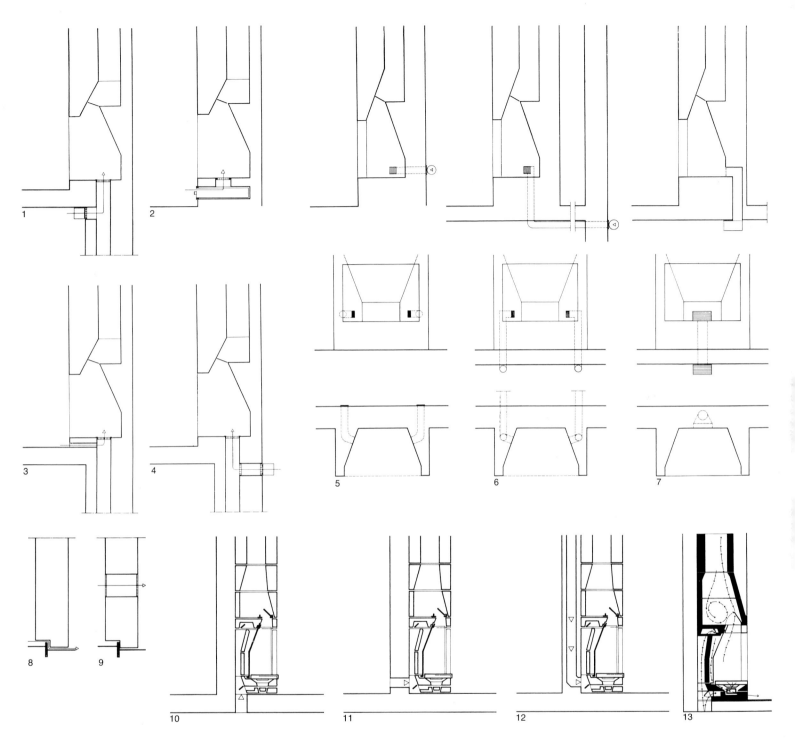

1–9. Verschiedene Formen der Luftzuführung. (Abb. 1: Luftzuführung aus dem Keller über den Aschenfallschacht; Abb. 2: Luftzuführung durch einen Schlitz in der Aschenschublade; Abb. 3: Luftzuführung durch einen Schlitz im Kaminsockel; Abb. 4: Luftzuführung aus dem Freien über den Aschenfallschacht; Abb. 5: Luftzuführungskanal führt in der Kaminwand direkt ins Freie; Abb. 6: Luftzuführungskanal führt unter der Decke hängend ins Freie; Abb. 7: Luftzuführungskanal führt in den Keller, Luftentnahme im Bereich des Untergeschosses;

Abb. 8: die normale Bewegungstoleranz einer Tür genügt oft für eine ausreichende Luftzuführung; Abb. 9: besser ist es, im unteren Bereich der Tür Luftschlitze oder -löcher auszuschneiden.)

10–13. Beispiele für die Luftzuführung beim Kamineinsatz „Superfire" der Firma Kaminbau Burgers Söhne, Thörishaus/Bern. (Abb. 10: die Zuluft wird im Keller, unmittelbar unter dem Kamin gefaßt; Abb. 11: steht der Kamin an einer Außenwand, so kann die Frischluft auf der Kaminrückseite unmittelbar aus dem Freien zuge-

führt werden; Abb. 12: wird die Frischluft im Dachboden oder über Dach gefaßt, so führt man sie dem Feuer mit einem Kanal zu, der parallel zum Schornstein läuft; Abb. 13: Verlauf der Luftströme und Verbrennungsgase.)

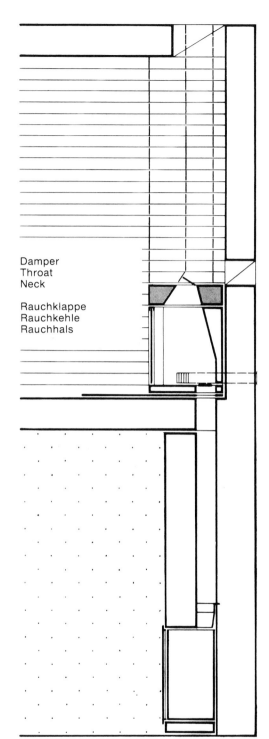

Damper
Throat
Neck

Rauchklappe
Rauchkehle
Rauchhals

## Neck/Throat/Damper

The neck, usually a funnel-shaped chamber tapering towards the top end, normally extends from the top edge of the fireplace opening to the throat. Its function is to suck up the smoke and to prevent smoke discharge into the room. Prefabricated neck units of fireclay or iron plate are recommended. Shape and arrangement depend on the construction of the firebox back wall and the position of the chimney. Alternatives:
a) Chimney above the firebox (figs. 1–3): The neck is run up 15–20 cm above the top edge of the fireplace opening to the smoke shelf; the front should ideally be tilted more than 60° horizontally.
b) Chimney above the firebox, but smoke shelf omitted (figs. 6, 7): The neck as direct, tapering passageway from the firebox to the chimney. It is advisable to retain the forward slope of the firebox back wall and slope up from the throat to the chimney.
c) Chimney behind or at the side of the firebox (figs. 10–13): Stove-like link, since the tapering neck discharges as smoke flue to the chimney, whereby the smoke shelf may be omitted. The upper part of the neck terminates in the throat, which together with the suction funnel of the neck, increases the velocity of flow by reducing the cross-section of the firebox (length of throat = approximate width of fireplace opening A, depth however only 10–20 cm. In any case, larger surface area than chimney cross-section). The damper, made almost exclusively of iron, which regulates the draught and shuts off the fireplace when the latter is not in use, is generally installed in the throat at the level of the smoke shelf (may also be installed in the smoke chamber or smoke flue). The many standardized dampers are classified in the following basic types: tiltable, swivelling or in the form of a draw plate. Each regulating rod must be lockable at various points. Complicated spring rods and gear transmissions are prone to defect. As a rule, fireplaces without a damper only function satisfactorily under favourable weather conditions, those with a stove-like connection better than others.

## Rauchhals/Rauchkehle/Rauchklappe

Der Rauchhals, ein sich meistens trichterförmig nach oben verjüngender Hohlraum, reicht normalerweise von Oberkante Feueröffnung bis zur Rauchkehle. Er hat die Aufgabe, den Rauch abzusaugen und Rauchausschlag zu verhindern. Empfehlenswert sind vorgefertigte Rauchhalseinsätze aus Schamotte oder Eisenblech. Form und Anordnung hängen von der Ausbildung der Feuerrückwand und der Lage des Schornsteins ab. Möglichkeiten:
a) Schornstein über der Feuerstelle (Abb. 1–3): Hochführen des Rauchhalses 15-20 cm über Oberkante Feueröffnung bis zum Rauchsims, Vorderseite am besten mehr als 60° zur Waagrechten geneigt.
b) Schornstein über der Feuerstelle, jedoch Verzicht auf Rauchsims (Abb. 6, 7): Der Rauchhals als direkter, sich verjüngender Übergang vom Feuerraum zum Schornstein. Es empfiehlt sich, die Schrägstellung der Feuerraumrückwand beizubehalten und von der Rauchkehle an zum Schornstein zu verziehen.
c) Schornstein neben oder hinter der Feuerstelle (Abb. 10–13): Ofenähnlicher Anschluß, da der sich verjüngende Rauchhals in Rauchkanal zum Schornstein übergeht, dabei Rauchsims nicht unbedingt erforderlich.
Der Rauchhals wird oben durch die Rauchkehle abgeschlossen, die zusammen mit dem Absaugtrichter des Rauchhalses durch Flächenverengung gegenüber dem Feuerraumquerschnitt eine höhere Strömungsgeschwindigkeit bewirkt (Länge der Rauchkehle = etwa Feueröffnungsbreite A, Tiefe jedoch nur 10–20 cm. In jedem Fall größerer Flächeninhalt als Schornsteinquerschnitt). Die fast immer aus Eisen bestehende Rauchklappe, die den Zug reguliert und den Kamin bei Nichtbenutzung schließt, wird meist in Höhe des Rauchsimses in die Rauchkehle eingebaut (Anordnung in Rauchkammer oder Rauchrohr gleichfalls möglich). Die zahlreichen serienmäßigen Rauchklappen lassen sich in folgende Grundtypen unterteilen: kippbar, drehbar oder als Zugschild ausgebildet. Jede Regulierstange muß sich unbedingt in verschiedenen Stellungen arretieren lassen. Komplizierte Federzugstangen und Zahnradübersetzungen sind störungsanfällig. Kamine ohne Rauchklappe funktionieren meist nur bei günstiger Witterung einwandfrei, am ehesten bei ofenähnlichem Anschluß.

1–13. Neck constructions. (Fig. 1: with skewing side walls; fig. 2: with parallel side walls; fig. 3: parallel side walls in very large fireplace opening, rectangular chimney cross-section, or solutions without a smoke chamber; figs. 4, 5: prefabricated necks of cast-iron plate with built-in damper; fig. 6: neck as direct passageway from the firebox to the chimney; fig. 7: improvement of example 6 through forward-sloping firebox back wall – excellently functioning solution when the chimney is arranged at the side of or behind the firebox; fig. 8: neck of a freestanding fireplace with large fireplace opening; fig. 9: large neck for fireplace with large three-sided opening and lateral smoke-flue link; fig. 10: neck construction with stove-like link to the chimney, smoke shelf and smoke chamber omitted; fig. 11: fireplace without neck; fig. 12: neck construction of a fireplace with smoke shelf and chimney behind the firebox; fig. 13: neck with vertical front wall and sloping back wall, chimney arranged behind the firebox.)
14–24. Dampers. (Fig. 14: tilting damper; fig. 15: swivelling damper; fig. 16: drawing damper; fig. 17: detailed drawing from example 4; fig. 18: detailed drawing from example 5; fig. 19: draught deflector; fig. 20: tilting damper with regulating rod lying within; fig. 21: tilting damper with external regulating handle; fig. 22: swivel damper; fig. 23: swivel damper with neck as built-in element; fig. 24: damper in the form of a draw plate.)

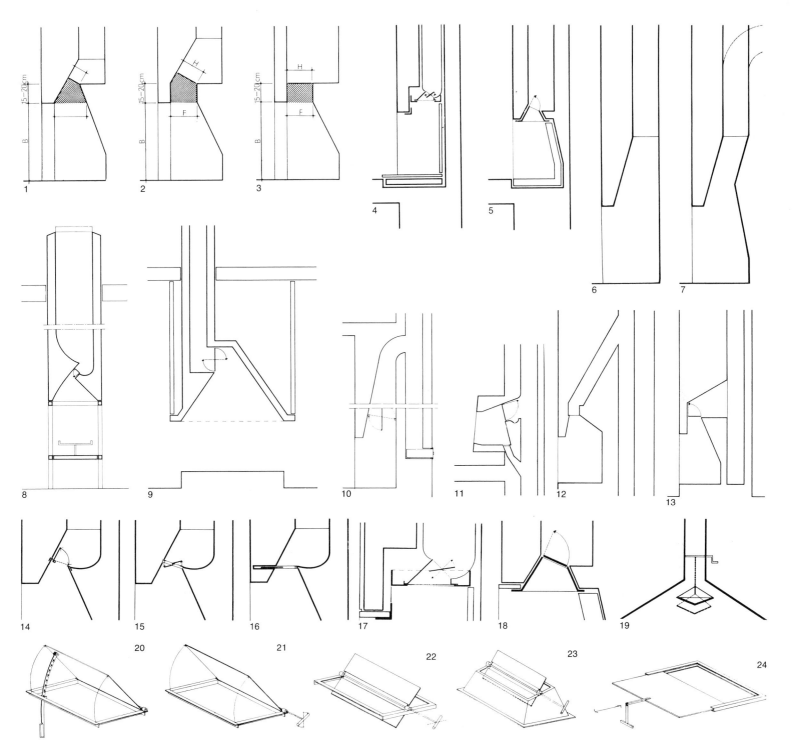

1–13. Rauchhalskonstruktionen. (Abb. 1: mit schrägen Seitenwänden; Abb. 2: mit parallelen Seitenwänden; Abb. 3: parallele Seitenwände bei sehr großer Feueröffnung, rechteckigem Schornsteinquerschnitt oder Lösungen ohne Rauchkammer; Abb. 4, 5: vorgefertigte Rauchhälse aus Eisenblech mit eingebauter Rauchklappe; Abb. 6: direkter Übergang des Rauchhalses vom Feuerraum zum Schornstein; Abb. 7: durch Schrägneigung der Feuerraumrückwand verbesserte Ausführung von Beispiel 6 – wenn Schornstein neben oder hinter der Feuerstelle angeordnet, ausgezeichnet funktionierende Lösung; Abb. 8: Rauchhals eines freistehenden Kamins mit großer Feueröffnung; Abb. 9: großer Rauchhals für Kamin mit großer, dreiseitiger Feueröffnung und seitlichem Rauchrohranschluß; Abb. 10: Rauchhalsausbildung bei Wegfall von Rauchsims und Rauchkammer sowie ofenähnlichem Anschluß an den Schornstein; Abb. 11: Kamin ohne Rauchhals; Abb. 12: Rauchhalsausbildung bei einem Kamin mit Rauchsims und Schornstein hinter der Feuerstelle; Abb. 13: Rauchhals mit gerader Vorder-
und geneigter Rückwand, Schornstein hinter der Feuerstelle angeordnet.)
14–24. Rauchklappen. (Abb. 14: Rauchklappe zum Kippen; Abb. 15. zum Drehen; Abb. 16. zum Ziehen; Abb. 17: Detail aus Beispiel 4; Abb. 18: Detail aus Beispiel 5; Abb. 19: Zug-Deflektor; Abb. 20: Rauchklappe zum Kippen mit innenliegender Regulierstange; Abb. 21: Rauchklappe zum Kippen mit außenliegendem Reguliergriff; Abb. 22: Drehklappe; Abb. 23: Drehklappe mit Rauchhals als Einbauelement; Abb. 24: Rauchklappe als Zugschild ausgebildet.)

29

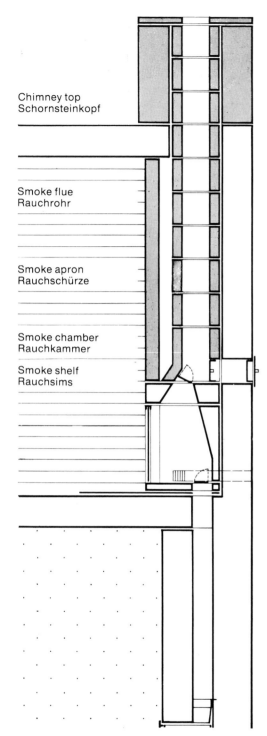

Chimney top
Schornsteinkopf

Smoke flue
Rauchrohr

Smoke apron
Rauchschürze

Smoke chamber
Rauchkammer

Smoke shelf
Rauchsims

## Smoke shelf/Smoke chamber/Chimney/Chimney top

The smoke shelf (figs. 1–4), which lies level with the throat, is formed by the forward sloping firebox back wall (about 20 cm above the upper edge of the fireplace opening). It is normally 10–20 cm wide and has in most cases a synclinical shape. Its function is to collect the soot falling from the chimney and, together with the smoke chamber, arrest the descending current of cold air. It is cleaned either through the throat via the firebox, or more comfortably, through a cleanout door in the back wall of the smoke chamber.

The smoke chamber (figs. 5–7) is a hollow space, shaped like an asymmetrical truncated pyramid, which provides the link between the neck and the chimney. It serves as pressure chamber to "reverse" the descending cold air, but above all, it is a smoke reservoir which prevents smoke and flames entering the room by sudden downwind. Side walls and front wall should ideally be sloped up at an angle of 60° or more, from the horizontal, to the chimney connection.

The cross-section of the chimney (figs. 8–15) has a specific dependent relationship with the selected size of the fireplace opening (see table on page 16): as a rule, it is 1/10 the area of the fireplace opening, by a chimney height of 6–12 m. The circular flue form is aerodynamically the most favourable, the square flue form the most frequent (in spite of causing swirls in the corners). The rectangular cross-section is unfavourable since strong swirls are hereby unavoidable. It goes without saying that no additional heating outlets may be connected to the fireplace chimney.

The chimney top (figs. 16–24) extends above the roof area and projects, next to the ridge, 50–70 cm beyond the edge of the ridge; below the ridge, its upper edge should be separated at least 1,50 m horizontally from the roof pane. In the case of flat roofs, the height of the chimney is 1–1,50 m.

1, 2. Gas-flow pattern of a fireplace with and without smoke shelf, each with chimney arranged centrally above the firebox. The smoke shelf or „deflection shelf" (fig. 1) reverses the descending cold air so that it is carried up through the flue, together with the ascending warm air, and discharged to the exterior. If the smoke shelf has been omitted (fig. 2), the cold air penetrates down to the firebox, causing the fire to flame up and smoke to issue into the room (according to W. Häusler, *Cheminée-Handbuch*).
3–7. Forms of construction for smoke shelf and smoke chamber. (Fig. 3: a frequently adopted smoke-shelf solution with double-walled cleanout door in the back wall of the smoke chamber; fig. 4: fireplace with centrally arranged chimney, no smoke shelf – very prone to disturbance; figs. 5, 6: view and section of a fireplace with one-sided fireplace opening and centrally arranged chimney; fig. 7: the first 50 cm or more

## Rauchsims/Rauchkammer/Schornstein/Schornsteinkopf

Der Rauchsims (Abb. 1–4), der in Höhe der Rauchkehle liegt, wird durch die vorgezogene Feuerraumrückwand (etwa 20 cm über Oberkante Feueröffnung) gebildet. Normalerweise ist er 10–20 cm breit und meist muldenförmig ausgeformt. Er soll den Ruß aus dem Schornstein sammeln und, in Verbindung mit der Rauchkammer, einfallende Kaltluft auffangen. Die Reinigung erfolgt entweder über den Feuerraum durch die Rauchkehle oder bequemer durch eine Putztür in der Rückwand der Rauchkammer.

Die Rauchkammer (Abb. 5–7) ist ein Hohlraum in Form eines asymmetrischen Pyramidenstumpfes, der die Verbindung zwischen dem Rauchhals und dem Schornstein herstellt. Sie dient als Staukammer bei der „Umkehrung" einfallender Kaltluft, vor allem aber ist sie Rauchreservoir, das bei plötzlichem Windeinfall Rauch- und Feuerrückschlag ins Zimmer verhütet. Seitenwände und Vorderwand werden am günstigsten in einem Winkel von 60° oder mehr, bezogen auf die Waagrechte, zum Schornsteinanschluß hochgeführt.

Der Querschnitt des Schornsteins (Abb. 8–15) steht in einem bestimmten Abhängigkeitsverhältnis zur gewählten Feueröffnungsgröße (siehe Tabelle auf Seite 16): in der Regel beträgt er 1/10 der Feueröffnungsfläche bei 6–12 m Schornsteinhöhe. Strömungstechnisch am günstigsten ist die runde Rauchrohrform, am häufigsten die quadratische (trotz Wirbelbildung in den Ecken). Ungünstig, da starke Wirbel unvermeidbar, ist der rechteckige Querschnitt. Selbstverständlich dürfen keine weiteren Feuerstellen an den Kaminschornstein angeschlossen werden.

Der Schornsteinkopf (Abb. 16–24) ragt über die Dachfläche hinaus und übersteigt in Firstnähe die Firstkante meist um 50–70 cm; unterhalb des Firsts sollte seine Oberkante mindestens 1,50 m in der Waagrechten von der Dachschräge entfernt sein. Bei Flachdächern beträgt die Schornsteinhöhe 1–1,50 m.

of the smoke flue above the smoke chamber must be strictly vertical before it may be sloped toward the horizontal at an angle of not less than 60°.)
8–15. Forms of construction for chimneys with circular and square flue cross-section. (Fig. 8: prefabricated chimney; fig. 9: chimney with brickwork mantle and smoke flue of hardburned clay; fig. 10: chimney with tubular shell of asbestos cement, insulation and „Iso" smoke flue; fig. 11: chimney with tubular shell of copper, insulation, and smoke flue of iron plate; fig. 12: prefabricated chimney; fig. 13: chimney with brickwork mantle and smoke flue with plaster facing; fig. 15: chimney with exterior brickwork mantle, air space, interior brickwork mantle and smoke flue with plaster facing.)
16–24. Forms of construction for chimney tops. (Fig. 16: brickwork capping; fig. 17: straight, low concrete cap; fig. 18: high, conical concrete cap; fig. 19: concrete pot, open at two sides; fig.

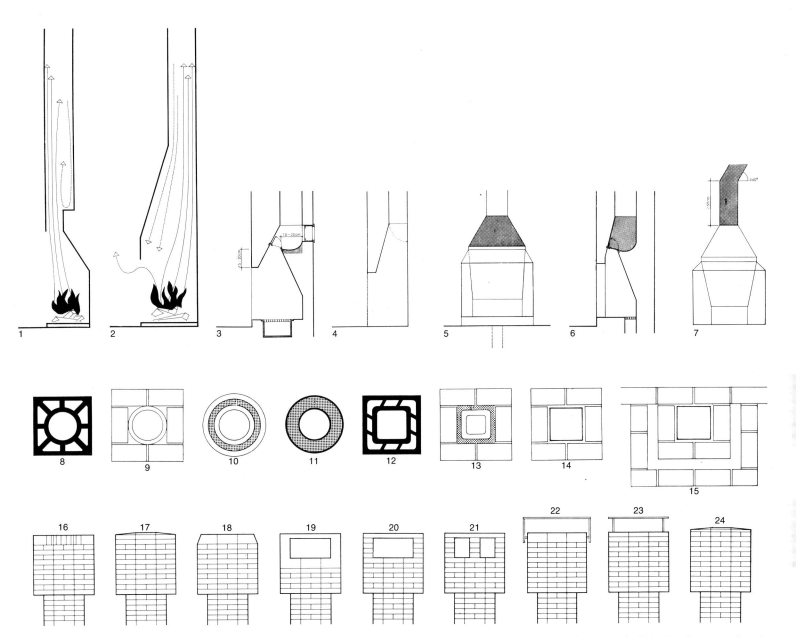

20: two lateral openings, brickwork, with concrete cap; fig. 21: four lateral openings, brickwork, with concrete cap; fig. 22: shield plate, with side attachment; fig. 23: shield plate, superimposed; fig. 24: steel cap.)

1, 2. Gasströmungsbild eines Kamins mit und ohne Rauchsims, jeweils mit zentral über der Feuerstelle angeordnetem Schornstein. Der Rauchsims oder „Umkehrboden" (Abb. 1) kehrt die einfallende Kaltluft um, so daß sie mit der aufsteigenden Warmluft durch den Schornstein ins Freie geleitet wird. Fehlt der Rauchsims (Abb. 2), so dringt die Kaltluft bis zur Feuerstelle herab, wo sie Flammenüberschlag und Rauchaustritt bewirkt (nach: W. Häusler, *Cheminée-Handbuch*).
3–7. Ausführungsbeispiele für Rauchsims und Rauchkammer. (Abb. 3: eine häufig angewandte Rauchsimslösung mit doppelwandiger Reini-

gungstür in der Rauchkammerrückwand; Abb. 4: Kamin ohne Rauchsims mit zentral angeordnetem Schornstein – sehr störungsanfällig; Abb. 5, 6: Ansicht und Schnitt eines Kamins mit einseitiger Feueröffnung und zentraler Schornsteinanordnung; Abb. 7: das Rauchrohr muß mindestens 50 cm über der Rauchkammer senkrecht hochgeführt werden, ehe es unter einem Winkel von nicht weniger als 60° zur Waagrechten verzogen werden darf.)
8–15. Ausführungsbeispiele für Schornsteine mit rundem und quadratischem Rauchrohrquerschnitt. (Abb. 8: Formschornstein; Abb. 9: Schornstein mit gemauertem Mantel und Rauchrohr aus hartgebranntem Ton; Abb. 10: Schornstein mit Mantelrohr aus Asbestzement, Isolierung und „Iso"-Rauchrohr; Abb. 11: Schornstein mit Mantelrohr aus Kupferblech, Isolierung und Rauchrohr aus Eisenblech; Abb. 12: Formschornstein; Abb. 13: Schornstein mit gemauertem Mantel, Vermiculite-Isolierung und

„Plewa"-Rauchrohr; Abb. 14: Schornstein mit gemauertem Mantel und Rauchrohrverputz; Abb. 15: Schornstein mit äußerem gemauertem Mantel, Luftraum, innerem gemauertem Mantel und Rauchrohrverputz.)
16–24. Ausführungsbeispiele für Schornsteinköpfe. (Abb. 16: gemauerte Abdeckung; Abb. 17: gerade, niedrige Betonabdeckplatte; Abb. 18: hohe, konische Betonabdeckplatte;; Abb. 19: zweiseitig offener Betonaufsatz; Abb. 20: zwei seitliche Öffnungen, gemauert, mit Betonabdeckplatte; Abb. 21: vier seitliche Öffnungen, gemauert, mit Betonabdeckplatte; Abb. 22: seitlich befestigte Schildplatte; Abb. 23: aufgesetzte Schildplatte; Abb. 24: Blechabdeckung.)

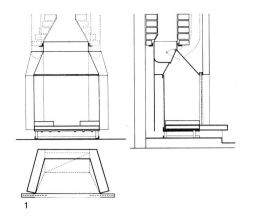

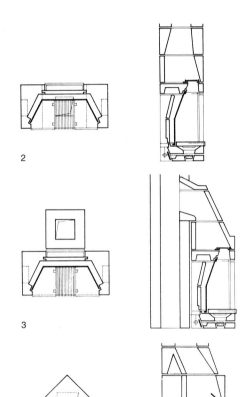

1

2

3

4

## Prefabricated fireplace elements

To facilitate as well as reduce the cost of fireplace construction, industry has developed standard prefabricated fireplace elements and built-in units. These may be used for any normal fireplace (as single parts or in combination with the basic construction), predominantly as prefabricated parts for the inner fireplace structure. Hereby, sufficient scope remains for the individual design of the exterior mantle. Specialist firms offer the following prefabricated elements for fireplace construction:

a) Of fireclay: hearths with and without firebridge, firebox side and back walls, neck lintels with and without recess for mounting the damper, necks with built-in damper of iron plate, smoke shelves, chimneys, ash-dump lids.

b) Of iron plate or cast iron: necks with built-in damper, dampers with mounting frame and regulating rod, damper plates, ash-dump lids and grates, various devices for ash removal and ash boxes, fire grates and andirons, air grids or dampers with and without ventilator.

Standardized fireplace units simplify the job of the architect and also the mason. In addition, they are usually cheaper than those manufactured individually. The industrially prefabricated units are divided into two groups:

a) Fireplace units for ordinary fireplaces with complete inner construction.

b) Fireplace units with air-heating chambers for additional warm-air heating. The effective heat emission of an ordinary fireplace is, as already mentioned, relatively low in comparison with other heating systems, even under favourable conditions. An increase of about 10–20% in the transmission of heat may (according to Häusler) be achieved through installing air-heating chambers. This way, the room is warmed by directly radiated heat (to a lesser extent) as well as by the circulating warm air. Hereby, fresh air (air from the out of doors) or recirculated air (room air) is drawn in from around the fireplace opening, approximately at floor level. This is then forced through the air chamber, which forms a cavity behind the back wall of the firebox, frequently behind the side walls at the same time, is strongly heated and recirculated as warm air to the upper area of the room through warm-air ducts. Through the installation of a regulating damper in the partition between the air chamber and the firebox, the fire may also be supplied with fresh air in the process. Since the construction of such a device is both complicated and expensive, the utilization of prefabricated fireplace units is recommended. In this case, the external design may, for the greater part, be carried out according to individual conceptions.

## Vorgefertigte Kaminelemente

Zur Erleichterung und Verbilligung der handwerklichen Ausführung des offenen Kamins wurden von der Industrie serienmäßig vorfabrizierte Kaminfertigteile und Einbauelemente entwickelt. Diese können für jeden beliebigen Normalkamin (als Einzelstücke oder mit der Grundkonstruktion kombiniert) verwendet werden. Es handelt sich hierbei vorwiegend um Fertigteile für die Innenkonstruktion. Für die individuelle Gestaltung des äußeren Mantels bleibt dabei noch genügend Spielraum erhalten. Der Fachhandel bietet folgende Fertigteile an:

a) Aus Schamotte: Feuerböden mit und ohne Feuerbock, Feuerraumseiten- und -rückwände, Rauchhalsstürze mit und ohne Aussparung für die Rauchklappenmontage, Rauchhälse mit eingebauter Rauchklappe aus Eisenblech, Rauchsimse, Schornsteine, Aschenfalldeckel.

b) Aus Eisenblech oder Gußeisen: Rauchhälse mit eingebauter Rauchklappe, Rauchklappen mit Einbaurahmen und Regulierstange, Rauchklappenschilde, Aschenfalldeckel und -roste, verschiedene Aschenfallkonstruktionen und Aschenbehälter, Feuerroste und Feuerböcke, Luftgitter oder Klappen mit und ohne Ventilator. Genormte Kamineinsätze erleichtern dem Architekten die Planungsarbeit und dem Kaminbauer das Versetzen. Sie liegen außerdem im Preis meist günstiger als in handwerklicher Einzelanfertigung hergestellte Kaminanlagen. Man unterscheidet bei den industriell gefertigten Einsätzen zwei Gruppen:

a) Kamineinsätze für einfache Kamine mit kompletter Innenkonstruktion.

b) Kamineinsätze mit Luftheizkammern für eine zusätzliche Warmluftbeheizung. Die effektive Wärmeabgabe eines einfachen Kamins ist, wie schon erwähnt wurde, selbst bei günstigsten Voraussetzungen gegenüber anderen Heizsystemen relativ gering. Eine Steigerung der Wärmeabgabe um etwa 10–20 % ist (nach Häusler) durch die Anordnung von Luftheizkammern möglich. Auf diese Weise wird der Raum sowohl durch die direkte Strahlungswärme, deren Anteil bei diesem Verfahren jedoch etwas zurückgeht, als auch durch die Warmluftzirkulation erwärmt. Hierbei wird Frischluft (Luft aus dem Freien) oder Umluft (Raumluft) im unteren Bereich neben der Feuerstelle, ungefähr in Höhe des Zimmerbodens, angesaugt. Diese Luft strömt dann durch die Luftkammer, die einen Hohlraum hinter der Feuerraumrückwand, oft aber auch gleichzeitig hinter den Feuerraumseitenwänden bildet, wird dabei stark erwärmt und durch Warmluftkanäle dem Raum im oberen Bereich als Warmluft wieder zugeführt. Durch den Einbau einer Regulierklappe in der Trennwand zwischen Luftkammer und Feuerraum, unmittelbar über oder unter dem Feuerboden, kann das Feuer auf diesem Wege außerdem noch mit Frischluft versorgt werden. Da die handwerkliche Ausführung einer solchen Anlage kompliziert und kostspielig ist, wird die Verwendung vorfabrizierter Kamineinsätze empfohlen. Die äußere Gestaltung kann dabei noch weitgehend nach individuellen Vorstellungen ausgeführt werden.

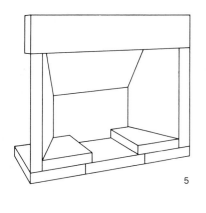

5

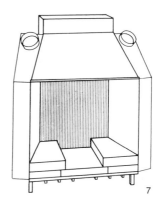

6

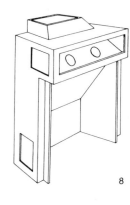

7

8

9

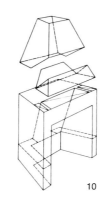

10

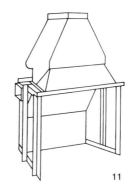

11

12

1. Constructional drawing of the "LU-NO-Warmluft-Feuerraum AHZ" from the company Cheminée Honegger, Zurich.

2–4. Constructional drawings of the various types of "Superfire" fireplace unit from the company Kaminbau Burgers Söhne, Thörishaus/Bern. (Fig. 2: with smoke flue to the top; fig. 3: with smoke flue to the rear; fig. 4: as corner fireplace.)

5. "Norm-Cheminée-Feuerraum AHZ" from the company Cheminée Honegger. Hearth and walls of fireclay slabs; smoke hood of steel plate. The fireplace unit may also be supplied open at two sides under the name "Norm-2-S".

6. Fireplace unit "Superfire" from the company Kaminbau Burgers Söhne. Special refractory concrete with individual parts of iron and gray cast iron. Built-in air-heating chamber. Two basic types: series KD with firebox openings of 70 x 50 cm and series KN with firebox openings of 95 x 70 cm. KDS (KNS) with smoke flue to the top, KDH (KNH) with smoke flue to the rear, KDE (KNE) as corner fireplace, KDL (KNL) and KDR (KNR) with firebox open at two sides.

7. "LU-NO-Warmluft-Feuerraum AHZ" from the company Cheminée Honegger. Casing of iron plate with hearth and back wall of ribbed cast-iron plates; hearth slabs of fireclay. Four sizes. The fireplace unit may also be supplied open at two sides under the name "LU-NO-2-S".

8. Fireplace unit "Termator" from the company AB Termator, Stockholm. Steel plate. The cold air drawn in through the two bottom openings leaves as warm air through the four top openings.

9. Fireplace unit "Benefire" from the Vestal Manufacturing Co., Sweetwater, Tennessee. Steel plate. With air-heating chamber.

10. Standard fireplace unit with air-heating chamber, designed by Ernst Neufert.

11. Fireplace unit with warm-air chamber from the company Bähler & Co., Bern.

12. Fireplace unit from the company K. N. Schløsser Møller, Oslo. Gray cast iron. With air-heating chamber. Two models: N 55 and N 70.

1. Konstruktionszeichnung des "LU-NO-Warmluft-Feuerraums AHZ" der Firma Cheminée Honegger, Zürich.

2–4. Konstruktionszeichnungen verschiedener Typen des Kamineinsatzes "Superfire" der Firma Kaminbau Burgers Söhne, Thörishaus/Bern. (Abb. 2: mit Rauchabzug nach oben; Abb. 3: mit Rauchabzug nach hinten; Abb. 4: als Eckkamin.)

5. "Norm-Cheminée-Feuerraum AHZ" der Firma Cheminée Honegger. Boden und Wände aus Schamotteplatten; Abzugshaube aus Stahlblech. Der Kamineinsatz ist unter der Bezeichnung "Norm-2-S" auch zweiseitig offen lieferbar.

6. Kamineinsatz "Superfire" der Firma Kaminbau Burgers Söhne. Feuerfester Spezialbeton mit Einzelteilen aus Eisen und Grauguß. Eingebaute Luftheizkammer. Zwei Grundtypen: Serie KD mit Feuerraumöffnungen von 70 x 50 cm und Serie KN mit Feuerraumöffnungen von 95 x 70 cm. KDS (KNS) mit Rauchabzug nach oben, KDH (KNH) mit Rauchabzug nach hinten, KDE

(KNE) als Eckkamin, KDL (KNL) bzw. KDR (KNR) mit zweiseitig offenem Feuerraum.

7. "LU-NO-Warmluft-Feuerraum AHZ" der Firma Cheminée Honegger. Gehäuse aus Eisenblech mit Boden und Feuerraumrückwand aus gerippten Gußplatten; Bodenplatten aus Schamotte. Vier Größen. Der Kamineinsatz ist unter der Bezeichnung "LU-NO-2-S" auch zweiseitig offen lieferbar.

8. Kamineinsatz "Termator" der Firma AB Termator, Stockholm. Stahlblech. Die durch die beiden unteren Öffnungen aufgenommene Kaltluft tritt durch die vier oberen Öffnungen als Warmluft wieder aus.

9. Kamineinsatz "Benefire" der Vestal Manufacturing Co., Sweetwater, Tennessee. Stahlblech. Mit Luftheizkammer.

10. Norm-Kamineinsatz mit Luftheizkammer, entworfen von Ernst Neufert.

11. Kamineinsatz mit Warmluftkasten der Firma Bähler & Co., Bern.

12. Kamineinsatz der Firma K. N. Schlösser Møller, Oslo. Grauguß. Mit Luftheizkammer. Zwei Modelle: N 55 und N 70.

## Prefabricated fireplaces

Prefabricated fireplaces are serial-produced and consist of inner construction, exterior mantle, smoke-flue connection and smoke flue. They are installed as complete unit or connected to existing chimneys. The choice between freestanding and wall fireplaces is given here also. It is advisable to mount the unit after completion of the finishing and service work in order to prevent the risk of damage. Since prefabricated fireplaces are very easy to erect, they are particularly suitable for installation in old houses. A wide range of models in various materials and to some extent of excellent design is already available today. Nevertheless, prefabricated fireplaces are only suitable for serial manufacture when the size of the fireplace opening can be varied without affecting the aesthetic appearance.

1. Model "Mexico" from the company Richard Le Droff, Evry, France. Base of fossil stone; covering of clinker quarter-bricks.
2. Model "Mitan" from the company Richard Le Droff. Base, smoke hood and smoke flue of stainless or ordinary-strength steel; hearth of clinker quarter-bricks.
3. Model "Mercury" from the Majestic Company, Huntington, Indiana (here as special construction of the architect Helmut C. Schulitz). Entire construction of steel.
4. Model 110 from the company Handöl AB, Sundbyberg, Sweden. Fireplace construction of steel; hearth and back wall of soapstone; side walls of glass.
5. Model 210 from the company Handöl AB. Fireplace construction of steel; firebox lining of soapstone.
6. Model 310 from the company Handöl AB. Fireplace construction of steel; firebox lining of cast iron.
7. Model "Olympic Franklin" from the Washington Stove Works, Everett, Washington. Fireplace structure of cast iron; smoke flue of steel plate.
8. Model "Capilla" from the company Polinax, Barcelona. Entire construction of steel plate.
9. Model "Fyrtønden" (fire drum) from the company Rais Produkter, Holte, Denmark. Fireplace construction of steel; firebox lined with fireclay bricks.
10. Model 1 from the company Cubus/ID, Copenhagen. Fireplace construction of steel plate; firebox lined with fireclay bricks.
11. Model 2 from the company Cubus/ID. Constructed as Model 1.
12. Stove/Fireplace from the company Cubus/ID. Construction of steel plate.

1

4

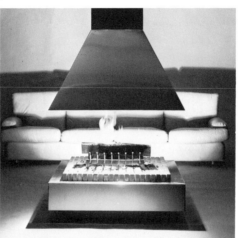

2

5

3

6

7

10

8

11

9

12

## Fertigkamine

Fertigkamine werden in Serie vorfabriziert und bestehen aus Innenkonstruktion, äußerem Mantel, Rauchrohranschluß und Rauchrohr. Sie werden als komplette Anlage installiert oder an vorhandene Schornsteine angeschlossen. Man kann auch in diesem Falle zwischen frei stehenden und Wandkaminen wählen. Die Montage erfolgt am besten nach Abschluß der Ausbauarbeiten, da so das Risiko einer Beschädigung vermieden wird. Da Fertigkamine sehr einfach aufzustellen sind, eignen sie sich besonders gut für den Einbau in Altbauwohnungen. Es steht heute bereits eine reichhaltige Auswahl an Modellen aus verschiedenen Materialien und teilweise in sehr guter Formgestaltung zur Verfügung. Vorgefertigte Kamine eignen sich aber nur dann zur Serienherstellung, wenn die Größe der Feueröffnung variiert werden kann, ohne daß dadurch die formale Erscheinung beeinträchtigt würde.

1. Modell „Mexico" der Firma Richard Le Droff, Evty, Frankreich. Sockel aus Fossilienstein; Abdeckung aus Klinkerriemchen.
2. Modell „Mitan" der Firma Richard Le Droff. Sockel, Rauchschirm und Rauchrohr aus Edel- oder Normalstahl; Feuertisch aus Klinkerriemchen.
3. Modell „Mercury" der Firma The Majestic Company, Huntington, Indiana (hier als Sonderkonstruktion des Architekten Helmut C. Schulitz). Gesamte Konstruktion aus Stahl.
4. Modell 110 der Firma Handöl AB, Sundbyberg, Schweden. Kaminkonstruktion aus Stahl; Feuertisch und Rückwand aus Speckstein; Seitenwände aus Glas.
5. Modell 210 der Firma Handöl AB. Kaminkonstruktion aus Stahl; Feuerraumauskleidung aus Speckstein.
6. Modell 310 der Firma Handöl AB. Kaminkonstruktion aus Stahl; Feuerraumauskleidung aus Gußeisen.
7. Modell „Olympic Franklin" der Firma Washington Stove Works, Everett, Washington. Kaminkörper aus Gußeisen; Rauchrohr aus Stahlblech.
8. Modell „Capilla" der Firma Polinax, Barcelona. Gesamte Konstruktion aus Stahlblech.
9. Modell „Fyrtønden" (Feuertonne) der Firma Rais Produkter, Holte, Dänemark. Kaminkonstruktion aus Stahl; Feuerraum mit Schamottesteinen ausgemauert.
10. Modell 1 der Firma Cubus/ID, Kopenhagen. Kaminkonstruktion aus Stahlblech; Feuerraum mit Schamottesteinen ausgemauert.
11. Modell 2 der Firma Cubus/ID. Konstruktion wie bei Modell 1.
12. Ofen/Kamin der Firma Cubus/ID. Konstruktion aus Stahlblech.

## Fireplace accessories

A wide range of fireplace accessories (fireside and cleaning tools as well as containers for transporting and storing wood) is available on the market today. Regrettfully, a tendency towards style imitation and pseudo applied art is becoming apparent in the formal design of many fireplace accessories.

The fireset consists of tongs, poker, shovel and brush, mostly made of iron or brass. They are usually hung on a freestanding dog or on a toolholder near the fire.

A small bellows with two handles is used for fanning the flames.

Baskets, buckets and containers are ideal for transporting wood and keeping a supply of logs near the fireplace. They should be sturdy but not too heavy, as hardwood in particular has considerable weight.

In recent years, grilling and frying on an open fireplace has become increasingly popular. For this purpose, simple grilldogs with gridirons and grilling devices with electrical or clockwork mechanism are available, as well as pan dogs for various types of pan and hooks for hanging up soup pots.

1. Fireset with freestanding toolholder.
2. Fireset with toolholder to be attached to the wall.
3. Bellows for fanning the flames.
4. Four-part fire screen.
5. Grill combination comprising gridiron, stand and hinged bracket (stand and hinged bracket patented). The hinged bracket widens the movement radius of the combination. A floor socket or clamping device may be supplied as attachment.
6. Removable grilling device with three spits.
(All devices from Cheminée Honegger, Zurich.)

## Kaminzubehör

Kaminzubehör (Schür- und Putzgeräte sowie Behälter für den Transport und die Aufbewahrung des Holzes) wird heute in reicher Auswahl angeboten. Um so bedauerlicher ist es, daß die formale Gestaltung bei vielen Kamingeräten eine stilimitierende und pseudo-kunstgewerbliche Tendenz zeigt.

Das Kaminbesteck besteht aus Feuerzange, Schürhaken, Kehrschaufel und Besen, meist aus Eisen oder Messing hergestellt. Die Geräte werden entweder an einem frei stehenden Bock oder an einem Gerätehalter in Nähe des Kamins aufgehängt.

Zum Anfachen des Feuers benutzt man einen kleinen Blasebalg mit zwei Handgriffen.

Zum Holztransport und zur Aufbewahrung eines Handvorrats eignen sich Körbe, Eimer und Traggestelle. Sie sollten zwar stabil, aber nicht allzu schwer sein, da vor allem Hartholz an sich schon ein beträchtliches Gewicht hat.

In den letzten Jahren erfreut sich das Grillen und Braten im offenen Kamin immer größerer Beliebtheit. Dafür gibt es einfache Bratböcke mit Grillrosten und Bratapparate mit elektrischem oder Uhrwerkantrieb, Pfannenböcke für verschiedene Arten von Pfannen und Kamingalgen zum Aufhängen von Suppenkesseln.

1. Kaminbesteck mit frei stehendem Gerätehalter.
2. Kaminbesteck mit an der Wand zu befestigendem Gerätehalter.
3. Blasebalg zum Anfachen des Feuers.
4. Vierteiliges Vorstellgitter.
5. Grill-Kombination, bestehend aus Grillrost, Säule und Gelenkarm (Säule und Gelenkarm patentrechtlich geschützt). Der Gelenkarm vergrößert den Bewegungsradius der Kombination. Als Befestigung sind eine Bodenhülse oder eine Klemmvorrichtung lieferbar.
6. Bratapparat zum Einbauen mit drei Spießen.
(Hersteller sämtlicher Geräte: Cheminée Honegger, Zürich.)

1

2

3

4

5

6

## Fuel

For the fireplaces shown in this book, wood is, almost exclusively, the only fuel which comes into question. Shape of flames, radiation of heat, intensity, noise and smell of burning depend on the following factors:

a) Type of wood. Hard woods (gross weight about 650 to 800 kg/m$^3$: maple, acacia, beech, oak and the wood of fruit trees) burn with quiet flames and leave little ash. The embers remain aglow for a long time. Soft woods (gross weight less than 650 kg/m$^3$: birch, chestnut, pine, poplar, elm) burn with lively flames and leave a lot of ash. The glow of the embers dies down quickly. Soft wood burns more quickly than hard wood, under equal conditions. Soft woods, in particular strongly resinous pine woods, frequently spatter sparks about when burning; for this reason, they should only be burned in fireplaces with appropriate protective devices.

b) Moisture. The firewood is best stored in such a way that its moisture content is almost equivalent to that of the atmosphere. Dried wood burns too quickly.

c) Size. The lenght of the logs conforms to the size of the firebox and the intended stacking. Long logs are preferable.

d) Stacking. Flat or oblique stacking arrangements, which can be varied in many forms, have proven very suitable. Hereby, it is important that the burning log permits free access of air from below, otherwise the fire will suffocate in ash. For this reason, the utilization of andirons is recommended. The first fire should be burned in the presence of the architect or builder.

## Brennmaterial

Als Brennmaterial kommt für die in diesem Buch gezeigten Kamine fast ausschließlich Holz in Frage. Flammenbild, Wärmeabgabe, Verbrennungsintensität, -geräusch und -geruch sind abhängig von folgenden Faktoren:

a) Holzart. Harthölzer (Rohwichte etwa 650 bis 800 kg/m$^3$: Ahorn, Akazie, Buche, Eiche, Obstbaumhölzer) brennen mit ruhiger Flamme und geben wenig Asche. Glutwärme hält lange an. Weichhölzer (Rohwichte geringer als 650 kg/m$^3$: Birke, Kastanie, Kiefer, Pappel, Tanne, Ulme) brennen mit lebhafter Flamme und geben viel Asche. Glut erlischt rasch. Unter gleichen Bedingungen verbrennt Weichholz schneller als Hartholz. Weichhölzer, besonders stark harzhaltige Nadelhölzer, sprühen häufig beim Verbrennen Funken aus, sie sollten deshalb nur in Kaminen mit entsprechenden Schutzvorrichtungen verwendet werden.

b) Feuchtigkeit. Die Lagerung des Brennholzes erfolgt am besten so, daß es ungefähr Luftfeuchtigkeit enthält. Ausgetrocknetes Holz verbrennt zu schnell.

c) Größe. Die Länge der Holzscheite richtet sich nach der Größe des Feuerraums und der beabsichtigten Schichtung. Lange Scheite sind vorzuziehen.

d) Schichtung. Gut bewährt haben sich die Flach- oder die Schrägschichtungen, die in vielen Formen variiert werden können. Wichtig ist dabei, daß sich den brennenden Scheiten von unten Luft zuführen läßt, sonst erstickt das Feuer in der Asche. Daher empfiehlt sich die Verwendung von Feuerböcken. Das erste Feuer sollte man in Gegenwart des Architekten oder Kaminbauers abbrennen.

1

1. Freestanding fireplace in a patio, combined with a pergola. Hearth slab of concrete; smoke hood and smoke flue of steel plate, suspended in the pergola construction. A downward tapering cone-shaped insert in the smoke hood serves to form a narrow circular damper slot and functions simultaneously as smoke shelf. Round bars are embedded in the outer edge of the hearth slab in which wind guards may be mounted. (House in Cuernavaca, Mexico, designed by Karl-Heinz Götz.)

1. Frei stehender Kamin in einem Wohnhof, kombiniert mit einer Pergola. Feuertisch aus Beton; Rauchschirm und Rauchrohr aus Stahlblech, eingehängt in die Pergolakonstruktion. Ein kegelförmiger, mit der Spitze nach unten weisender Einsatz im Rauchschirm dient zur Bildung eines umlaufenden schmalen Rauchkehlenschlitzes und zugleich als Rauchsims. Am äußeren Rand des Feuertischs sind Rundstäbe einbetoniert, auf die Windschutzplatten aufgesteckt werden können. (Haus in Cuernavaca, Mexiko, entworfen von Karl-Heinz Götz.)

2. Freestanding fireplace in a living room. Fireplace construction of aluminium. The hearth is fitted with a ring of air vents, so that the fire, in combination with an exhaust fan on the chimney, may be operated independently of the room air. The circular air supply and the suction reduce the danger of flying sparks so effectively, that the originally planned metal-texture curtain was omitted. The slender form of the fireplace complies with the desire to maintain a good view of the out of doors through the glass front. (Robert Wiley House, New Canaan, Connecticut, designed by Philip Johnson.)

2. Frei stehender Kamin in einem Wohnraum. Kaminkonstruktion aus Aluminium. Der Feuertisch ist kranzförmig mit Zuluftschlitzen ausgestattet, so daß die Anlage in Verbindung mit einem auf dem Schornstein sitzenden Exhaustor völlig unabhängig von der Raumluft betrieben werden kann. Die umlaufende Luftzuführung und die Absaugung vermindern die Gefahr des Funkenflugs so weit, daß auf einen ursprünglich vorgesehenen Vorhang aus Metallgewebe verzichtet werden konnte. Die schlanke Form des Kamins entsprang dem Wunsch, die Aussicht durch die Glaswand möglichst wenig zu behindern. (Robert Wiley House, New Canaan, Connecticut, entworfen von Philip Johnson.)

2

3, 4. Prefabricated fireplace hanging freely in a two-storey-high living room (model "Mercury" from The Majestic Company, Huntington, Indiana). Fireplace construction of steel plate. The fire area may be closed in by a two-part spark screen. The fireplace normally sits on a 36 cm high base, which has been omitted here in favour of the suspended construction. (House in Beverly Hills, California, designed by Helmut C. Schulitz.)

3, 4. Frei hängender Fertigkamin in einem zwei Geschoß hohen Wohnraum (Modell „Mercury" der Firma The Majestic Company, Huntington, Indiana). Kaminkonstruktion aus Stahlblech. Der Feuerraum kann durch ein zweiteiliges Funkenschutzgitter abgeschlossen werden. Im Normalfall sitzt der Kamin auf einem etwa 36 cm hohen Sockel, der hier wegen der vom Architekten vorgesehenen Hängekonstruktion entfallen konnte. (Haus in Beverly Hills, Kalifornien, entworfen von Helmut C. Schulitz.)

3

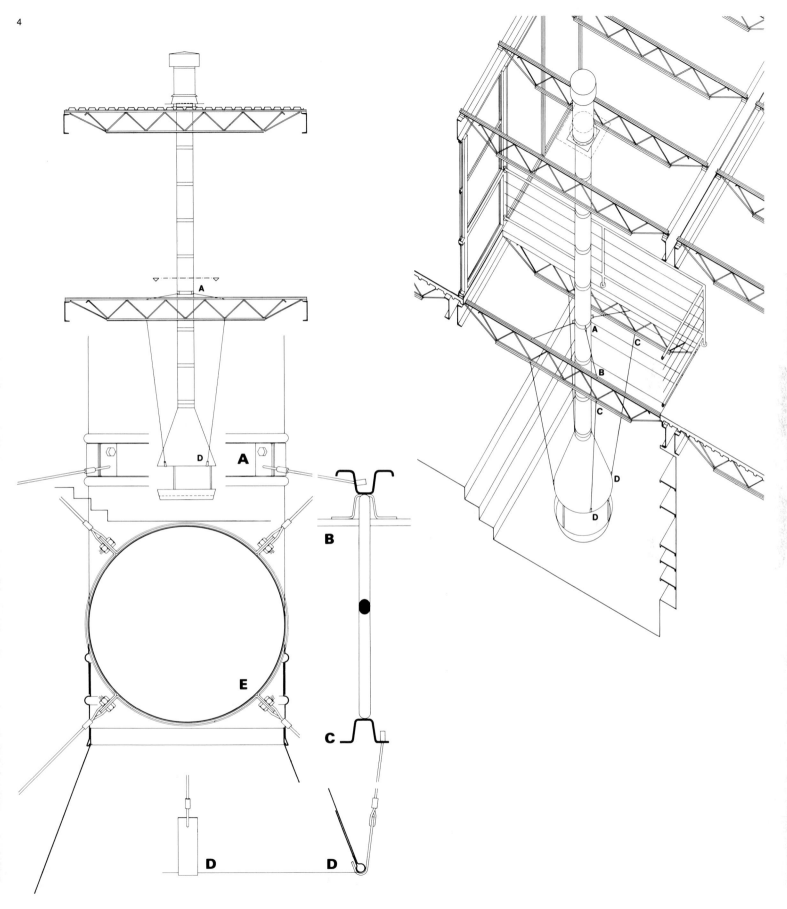

5

6

5, 6. Freestanding fireplace in the hall of a convalescent home. Hearth pit in brickwork; smoke hood and smoke flue of steel plate. A short distance from the hood, the smoke flue is attached to the timber wall behind. (Hiruzen Lodge, Hiruzen Highlands, Japan, designed by Takenaka Komuten Co., Ltd.)

7. Freestanding prefabricated fireplace (model "Mitan" from the company Richard Le Droff, Evry, France, designed by Jacques Le Guen). Base, smoke hood and smoke flue of brushed stainless steel or plain steel with rivets, painted black; hearth bed of brown-red watered clinker. The ash dump is fitted with an adjustable supply-air grid; the fire grate is removable.

7

5, 6. Frei stehender Kamin in der Halle eines Erholungsheims. Feuergrube in Ziegelmauerwerk; Rauchschirm und Rauchrohr aus Stahlblech. Das Rauchrohr ist mit einem kleinen Abstand an der dahinterliegenden Holzwand befestigt. (Hiruzen Resort Lodge, Hiruzen Highlands, Japan, entworfen von Takenaka Komuten Co., Ltd.)

7. Frei stehender Fertigkamin (Modell „Mitan" der Firma Richard Le Droff, Evry, Frankreich, entworfen von Jacques Le Guen). Sockel, Rauchschirm und Rauchrohr aus gebürstetem Edelstahl oder schwarz gestrichenem Normalstahl mit Nieten; Feuertisch aus braunrot geflammten Klinkerriemchen. Der Aschenfall ist mit einem regelbaren Zuluftgrill ausgestattet, der Feuerrost kann abgenommen werden.

8, 9. Freestanding fireplace in a two-storey-high living room. Base, fire grate, smoke hood and smoke flue of steel. The fireplace ist open at all sides; the fire grate, however, has been combined with a hood so that the fire itself is closed in at one side. (Erskine House, Drottningholm, Sweden, designed by Ralph Erskine.)

8, 9. Frei stehender Kamin in einem zwei Geschoß hohen Wohnraum. Sockel, Feuerrost, Rauchschirm und Rauchrohr aus Stahl. Der Kamin ist zwar allseits offen, der Feuerrost wurde jedoch mit einem Schirm kombiniert, der das Feuer halbseitig abdeckt. (Haus Erskine, Drottningholm, Schweden, entworfen von Ralph Erskine.)

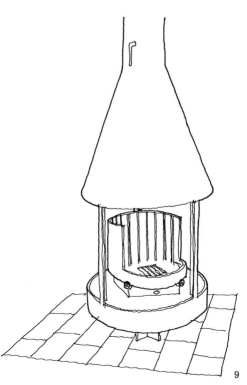

8

9

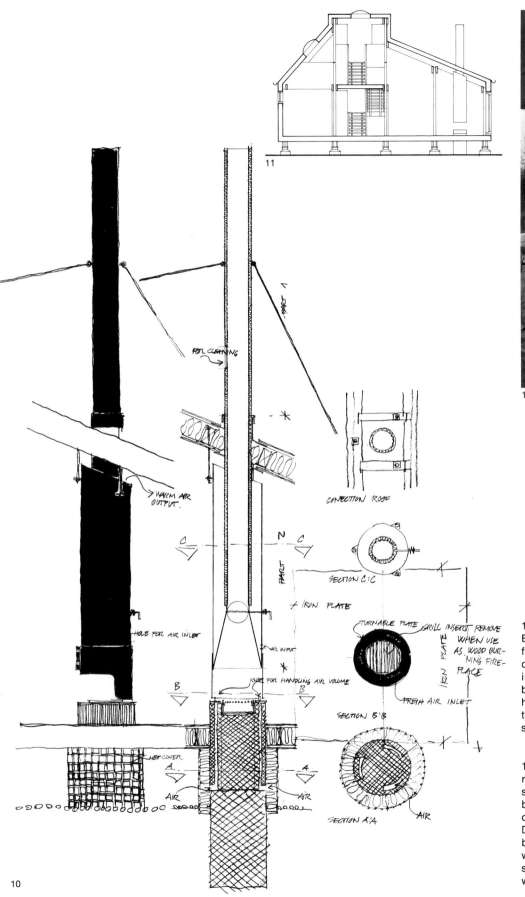

11

12

10

10–12. Freestanding fireplace in a living room. Base of concrete; smoke hood, apron, flue and facing of steel plate. The fire has a direct supply of fresh air through ducts which have been inserted in the base. The helmet-like hood can be rotated in every direction. The smoke flue has thermal insulation and is anchored above the roof. (Saks House, Helsingør, Denmark, designed by Bent Saks.)

10–12. Frei stehender Kamin in einem Wohnraum. Sockel aus Beton; Rauchschirm, Feuerschürze, Rauchrohr und Verkleidung aus Stahlblech. In den Sockel sind Kanäle eingelassen, die der Feuerstelle direkte Frischluft zuführen. Der helmartige Feuerschirm läßt sich in jede beliebige Richtung drehen. Das Rauchrohr ist wärmegedämmt und über dem Dach abgespannt. (Haus Saks, Helsingør, Dänemark, entworfen von Bent Saks.)

13–15. Freestanding fireplace in a living room. Fireplace construction of steel plate; connecting ring in the centre of the fireplace structure and bottom edge of hearth aperture of cast iron; hearth of cement. The aperture may be closed by a pivoting spark guard. The smoke flue is thermally insulated above the roof. (Gerald Frey House, designed by Wendell H. Lovett.)

13–15. Frei stehender Kamin in einem Wohnraum. Kaminkonstruktion aus Stahlblech; Verbindungsring in der Mitte des Kaminkörpers und unterer Rand der Feueröffnung aus Gußeisen; Feuerplatz aus Zement. Die Feueröffnung läßt sich mit einem drehbar gelagerten Funkenschutzgitter verschließen. Das Rauchrohr ist oberhalb des Daches wärmegedämmt. (Gerald Frey House, entworfen von Wendell H. Lovett.)

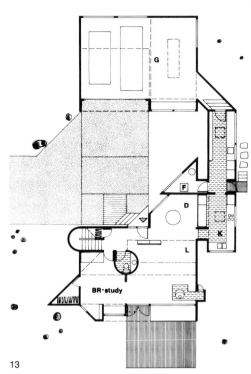

13

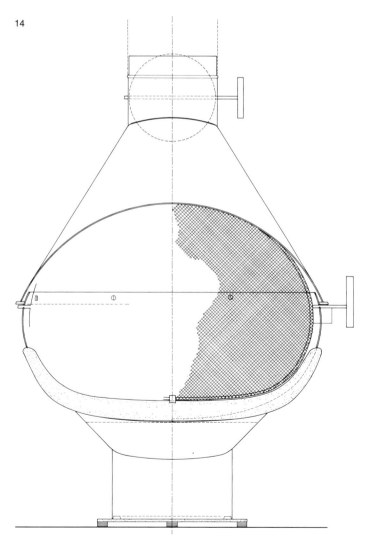

14

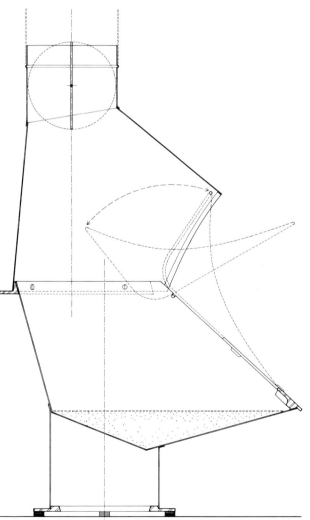

16. Fireplace standing in front of a medium-high partition wall in a living room. Fire surface of clinkers; fireplace construction of steel plate. The fireplace has been reduced to the bare necessities: firebridge, hood, smoke flue; it has neither a device for arresting descending air nor a damper. (Monahan House, Castlecrag, Australia, designed by Harry Seidler.)

16. Vor einer halbhohen Trennwand stehender Kamin in einem Wohnraum. Feuerfläche aus Klinkern; Kaminkonstruktion aus Stahlblech. Der Kamin ist auf das Allernotwendigste reduziert: Feuerbock, Haube, Rauchrohr; es gibt weder eine Vorrichtung zum Aufhalten von Falluft noch eine Rauchklappe. (Monahan House, Castlecrag, Australien, entworfen von Harry Seidler.)

17. Fireplace standing in front of a wall in a living room. Fireplace construction of steel plate, varnished. The fireplace stands on a slightly elevated floor of slabs. A light metal screen serves as spark guard. (Apartment in Boston, designed by Gerard R. Cugini Associates.)

17. Vor einer Wand stehender Kamin in einem Wohnraum. Kaminkonstruktion aus Stahlblech, lackiert. Der Kamin steht auf einem leicht erhöhten Plattenbelag. Als Funkenschutz dient ein leichtes Metallgitter. (Apartment in Boston, entworfen von Gerard R. Cugini Associates.)

17

18, 19. Prefabricated fireplace hanging in front of a wall in a living room (model "Capilla" from the company Polinax, Barcelona, designed by José Antonio Coderch y de Sentmenat). Fireplace construction of steel plate. The bars of the fire grate have been sloped up about 20 cm at the front to protect against flying sparks. (Casa Coderch, Epolla, Spain, designed by J. A. Coderch y de Sentmenat.)

18, 19. Vor einer Wand hängender Fertigkamin in einem Wohnraum (Modell „Capilla" der Firma Polinax, Barcelona, entworfen von José Antonio Coderch y de Sentmenat). Kaminkonstruktion aus Stahlblech. Zum Schutz gegen Funkenflug sind die Stäbe des Feuerrosts vorn etwa 20 cm hochgezogen. (Casa Coderch, Espolla, Spanien, entworfen von J. A. Coderch y de Sentmenat.)

18

19

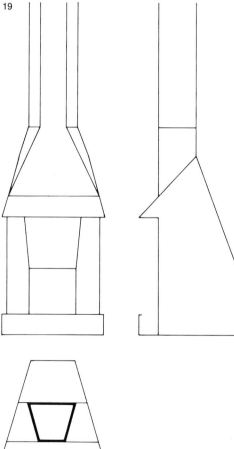

20. The model "Capilla" standing free in front of the window wall of a living room. Since a rear attachment was not possible here, the fireplace was connected to the floor by means of a thin metal pipe. A large metal slab protects the carpet against sparks. (Casa Tapies, Barcelona, designed by J. A. Coderch y de Sentmenat.)

20. Das Modell „Capilla" frei stehend vor einer Fensterwand in einem Wohnraum. Da hier eine rückseitige Befestigung nicht möglich war, wurde der Kamin durch ein dünnes Metallrohr mit dem Boden verbunden. Eine große Metallplatte schützt den Teppichboden gegen Funken. (Casa Tapies, Barcelona, entworfen von J. A. Coderch y de Sentmenat.)

20

21–23. Prefabricated fireplace (model "Tredos" from the company Rodon, Barcelona, Spain, designed by Martorell, Bohigas, Mackay) which may be situated in a corner (fig. 21) or stand free in the room (fig. 23). Fireplace construction of steel plate. The hearth is so large that even non-fireproof floor coverings may be run right up to the base of the fireplace. The fire grate can be lifted out of the ash box for removal of ash. (Fig. 23 residence in Barcelona, designed by Martorell, Bohigas, Mackay.)

21–23. Fertigkamin, wahlweise in eine Raumecke (Abb. 21) oder frei in den Raum (Abb. 23) zu stellen (Modell „Tredos" der Firma Rodon, Badalona, Spanien, entworfen von Martorell, Bohigas, Mackay). Kaminkonstruktion aus Stahlblech. Der Feuertisch ist so groß dimensioniert, daß auch brandempfindliche Bodenbeläge bis an den Kaminsockel herangeführt werden können. Der Feuerrost läßt sich zum Entfernen der Asche aus dem Aschenkasten abnehmen. (Abb. 23 Wohnhaus in Barcelona, entworfen von Martorell, Bohigas, Mackay.)

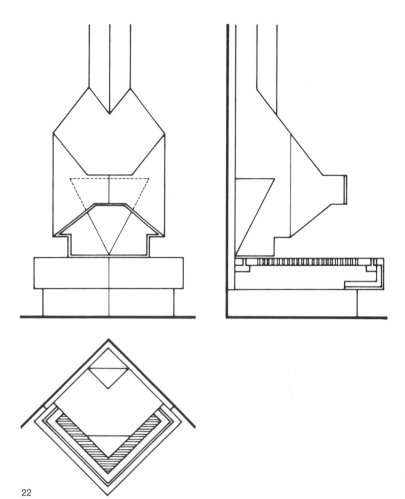

22

23

24–26. Prefabricated fireplace with choice of rear or top smoke-flue outlet, here as freestanding model in a two-storey-high living room (model "Olympic Franklin" from the Washington Stove Works, Everett, Washington). Fireplace structure of cast iron, from original moulds; smoke flue here of sheet metal with facing of stainless steel. The accessories available include a spark guard, a swing-out grill as well as a cooking pot with hanging fixture. To protect the carpet, this fireplace was mounted on a raised platform. (Private residence in Aptos Beach, California, designed by MLTW/Turnbull Associates.)

24–26. Fertigkamin, wahlweise mit rückwärtigem oder oberem Rauchrohrstutzen, hier frei stehend in einem zwei Geschoß hohen Wohnraum. (Modell „Olympic Franklin" der Firma Washington Stove Works, Everett, Washington). Kaminkörper aus Gußeisen, gegossen nach alten Formen; Rauchrohr hier aus Blech mit Edelstahlverkleidung. Als Zusatzteile sind unter anderem ein Funkenschutzgitter, ein ausschwenkbarer Grill sowie ein Kochtopf mit Hängevorrichtung erhältlich. Zum Schutz des Teppichbodens wurde der Kamin hier auf einem erhöhten Podest installiert. (Wohnhaus in Aptos Beach, Kalifornien, entworfen von MLTW/Turnbull Associates.)

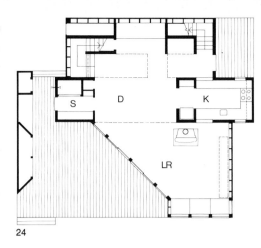

24

25

27

28

27-29. Prefabricated fireplaces (series 200 and 300 from the company Handöl AB, Sundbyberg, Sweden, designed by Lars Lallerstedt). Fireplace construction and floor plate of steel plate, enamelled; firebox lining of soapstone (series 200) or of cast iron (series 300). Grill units as well as an insert for heating with coal or briquettes, for both series, may be supplied additionally.
27. Model 310 for freestanding installation with complete chimney equipment.
28. Model 320 with bend pipe for connection to an existing chimney.
29. Model 210 for freestanding installation with complete chimney equipment (Model 220 corresponding to Model 320).

27-29. Fertigkamine (Serien 200 und 300 der Firma Handöl AB, Sundbyberg, Schweden, entworfen von Lars Lallerstedt). Kaminkonstruktion und Bodenplatte aus Stahlblech, lackiert; Feuerraumauskleidung aus Speckstein (Serie 200) bzw. aus Gußeisen (Serie 300). Für beide Serien sind zusätzlich Grilleinsätze sowie ein Einsatz zum Heizen mit Kohlen oder Briketts lieferbar.
27. Modell 310 für freie Aufstellung mit kompletter Schornsteinausrüstung.
28. Modell 320 mit Rohrkrümmer zum Anschluß an einen vorhandenen Schornstein.
29. Modell 210 für freie Aufstellung mit kompletter Schornsteinausrüstung (Modell 220 entsprechend Modell 320).

30–32. Freestanding fireplace in a two-storey-high living room. Fireplace construction of steel plate, enamelled. The fire area may be closed off by means of a tiltable spark guard balanced by a counterweight. The fireplace stands on a concrete base with a covering of bricks. (Donald Grish House, Enumclaw, Washington, designed by Wendell H. Lovett.)

30–32. Frei stehender Kamin in einem zwei Geschoß hohen Wohnraum. Kaminkonstruktion aus Stahlblech, lackiert. Der Feuerraum kann mit einem kippbaren, durch ein Gegengewicht ausbalancierten Funkenschutzgitter abgeschlossen werden. Der Kamin steht auf einem mit Ziegelsteinen belegten Betonsockel. (Donald Grish House, Enumclaw, Washington, entworfen von Wendell H. Lovett.)

31

30

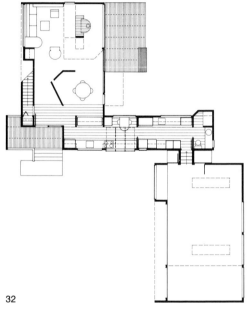

32

33. Fireplace standing free in front of a glass wall in a living room. Fireplace construction of steel plate, enamelled. A horizontally sliding metal curtain serves as spark guard. The fireplace stands on a washed concrete base. (William Wallace House, Mercer Island, Washington, designed by Wendell H. Lovett.)

33. Frei vor einer Fensterwand stehender Kamin in einem Wohnraum. Kaminkonstruktion aus Stahlblech, lackiert. Als Funkenschutz dient ein seitlich verfahrbarer Metallvorhang. Der Kamin steht auf einem Waschbetonsockel. (William Wallace House, Mercer Island, Washington, entworfen von Wendell H. Lovett.)

33

34–36. Fireplace standing free beside a book-case wall in a two-storey-high living room. Fireplace construction of steel profiles and steel plate, coated. The smoke flue is thermally insulated above the roof. A large ash drawer is located in the base. (Zobel House, Bad Herrenalb, Germany, designed by Karl-Heinz Götz.)

34–36. Frei neben einer Regalwand stehender Kamin in einem zwei Geschoß hohen Wohnraum. Kaminkonstruktion aus Stahlprofilen und Stahlblech, gestrichen. Das Rauchrohr ist oberhalb des Daches wärmedämmend verkleidet. Im Sockel befindet sich eine große Aschenschublade. (Haus Zobel, Bad Herrenalb, entworfen von Karl-Heinz Götz.)

35

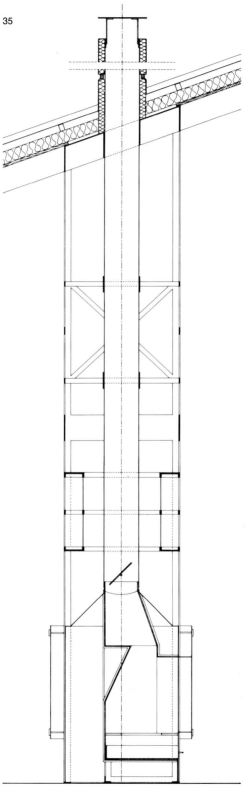

34

37

38

37, 38. Prefabricated fireplace, with choice of rear or upper smoke-flue outlet (Model "Fyrtønden" from the company Rais Produkter, Holte, Denmark, designed by Hans Dall). Fireplace construction of steel, hand-forged; firebox lined with fireclay bricks. The fire area can be closed by a vertically sliding plate; when closed, the "Fire drum" is an efficient wood stove. (Fig. 37 single-family house in Brabrand, Denmark, designed by Nils Primdahl & Erich Weitling.)

37, 38. Fertigkamin, wahlweise mit hinterem oder oberem Rauchrohrstutzen (Modell „Fyrtønden" der Firma Rais Produkter, Holte, Dänemark, entworfen von Hans Dall). Kaminkonstruktion aus Stahl, handgeschmiedet; Feuerraum mit Schamottesteinen ausgemauert. Der Feuerraum kann durch einen vertikal verfahrbaren Schild verschlossen werden; im geschlossenen Zustand ist die „Feuertonne" ein leistungsfähiger Holzofen. (Abb 37 Einfamilienhaus in Brabrand, Dänemark, entworfen von Nils Primdahl & Erich Weitling.)

39

40

39, 40. Prefabricated fireplace (Series 100 from the company Handöl AB, Sundbyberg, Sweden, designed by Lars Lallerstedt). Fireplace construction and floor plate of steel, enamelled; hearth and back wall of firebox of soapstone; side walls of glass. Accessories include a grill unit as well as an insert for heating with coal or briquettes. The fireplace, as shown here, may also be supplied with an upper part of soapstone; similarly, the glass may be replaced by soapstone. The feet may be cased with a steel-plate base. The fireplace may be supplied with complete chimney equipment (Model 110; fig. 39), with angled flue (Model 120) as well as rear flue (Model 130; fig. 40).

39, 40. Fertigkamin (Serie 100 der Firma Handöl AB, Sundbyberg, Schweden, entworfen von Lars Lallerstedt). Kaminkonstruktion und Bodenplatte aus Stahl, lackiert; Feuertisch und Feuerraumrückwand aus Speckstein; Seitenwände aus Glas. Als Zusatzteile gibt es einen Grilleinsatz sowie einen Einsatz zum Heizen mit Kohlen oder Briketts. Wie hier gezeigt, ist der Kamin auch mit einem Oberteil aus Speckstein erhältlich; ebenso kann das Glas gegen Speckstein ausgewechselt werden. Die Beine lassen sich mit einem Blechsockel verkleiden. Der Kamin ist mit kompletter Schornsteinausrüstung (Modell 110; Abb. 39), mit abgewinkeltem Rauchabzug (Modell 120) sowie mit rückwärtigem Rauchabzug (Modell 130; Abb. 40) lieferbar.

41. Prefabricated fireplace combined with a log niche standing free in a living room (model "Polo" from the company Polinax, Barcelona, designed by José Antonio Coderch y de Sentmenat). Fireplace construction, ash box and floor plate of steel plate; fire grate of sectional steel. (Casa Tapies, Barcelona, designed by J. A. Coderch y de Sentmenat.)

42, 43. The model "Polo" hanging in front of a wall in a living room. (Fig. 42 house in Cadaques, Spain; fig. 43 Casa Coderch, Espolla, Spain; both designed by J. A. Coderch y de Sentmenat.)

41. Fertigkamin, frei in einem Wohnraum stehend, verbunden mit einer Holzlege (Modell „Polo" der Firma Polinax, Barcelona, entworfen von José Antonio Coderch y de Sentmenat). Kaminkonstruktion, Aschenkasten und Bodenblech aus Stahlblech; Feuerrost aus Stahlprofilen. (Casa Tapies, Barcelona, entworfen von J. A. Coderch y de Sentmenat.)

42, 43. Das Modell „Polo" hängend vor einer Wand in einem Wohnraum. (Abb. 42 Haus in Cadaques, Spanien; Abb. 43 Casa Coderch, Espolla, Spanien; beide entworfen von J. A. Coderch y de Sentmenat.)

42

43

44, 45. Prefabricated fireplace suspended on the wall (Fireplace 1 from the company Cubus/ID, Copenhagen, designed by Nils Fagerholt). Fireplace construction of steel plate; fire area lined with fireclay bricks. The flue outlet is normally located in the centre axis of the rear; the fireplace can, however, on request, be supplied with an outlet displaced approx. 23 cm to the left or right.

44, 45. Fertigkamin, an der Wand hängend (Kamin 1 der Firma Cubus/ID, Kopenhagen, entworfen von Nils Fagerholt). Kaminkonstruktion aus Stahlblech; Feuerraum mit Schamottesteinen ausgemauert. Der Rauchrohrstutzen sitzt normalerweise in der Mittelachse der Rückwand; der Kamin kann jedoch auf Wunsch auch mit einem um 23 cm nach links oder rechts versetzten Stutzen geliefert werden.

44

45

46

47

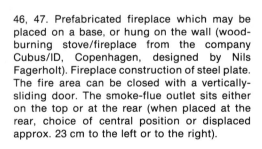

48. Prefabricated fireplace suspended on the wall (Fireplace 2 from the company Cubus/ID, Copenhagen, designed by Nils Fagerholt). Fireplace construction of steel plate; fire area lined with fireclay bricks. The fire area can be closed with two vertically-sliding doors.

48. Fertigkamin, an der Wand hängend (Kamin 2 der Firma Cubus/ID, Kopenhagen, entworfen von Nils Fagerholt). Kaminkonstruktion aus Stahlblech; Feuerraum mit Schamottesteinen ausgemauert. Der Feuerraum kann mit zwei seitlich angeschlagenen Türen verschlossen werden.

48

46, 47. Prefabricated fireplace which may be placed on a base, or hung on the wall (woodburning stove/fireplace from the company Cubus/ID, Copenhagen, designed by Nils Fagerholt). Fireplace construction of steel plate. The fire area can be closed with a vertically-sliding door. The smoke-flue outlet sits either on the top or at the rear (when placed at the rear, choice of central position or displaced approx. 23 cm to the left or to the right).

46, 47. Fertigkamin, wahlweise auf ein Untergestell zu stellen oder an die Wand zu hängen. (Ofen/Kamin der Firma Cubus/ID, Kopenhagen, entworfen von Nils Fagerholt). Kaminkonstruktion aus Stahlblech. Der Feuerraum kann mit einer vertikal verfahrbaren Tür verschlossen werden. Der Rauchabzugsstutzen sitzt entweder an der Ober- oder an der Rückseite (bei rückseitigem Sitz wahlweise mittig oder um 23 cm nach links bzw. rechts versetzt).

49–52. Fireplace standing in front of a wall in a two-storey-high living room. Fireplace construction of steel, varicoloured finish. Behind the outer hood, the actual upward-tapering smoke hood is concealed. The hearth consists of firebricks, the surrounding safety area of glass mosaic. (Max Scofield House, Mercer Island, Washington, designed by Wendell H. Lovett.)

49–52. Vor einer Wand stehender Kamin in einem zwei Geschoß hohen Wohnraum. Kaminkonstruktion aus Stahl, verschiedenfarbig lackiert. Hinter der äußeren Haube verbirgt sich der eigentliche, nach oben sich verjüngende Rauchschirm. Der Kaminboden besteht aus feuerfesten Ziegeln, der diesen umgebende Sicherheitsstreifen aus Glasmosaik. (Max Scofield House, Mercer Island, Washington, entworfen von Wendell H. Lovett.)

49

50

52

51

53, 54. Freestanding fireplace on the terrace of a residence. Fireplace construction of concrete, held between support and chimney; firebox lined with 35 mm thick fireclay slabs which have been attached to the concrete by means of strong screws. (Z House, Karlsruhe, designed by Reinhard Gieselmann.)

53, 54. Frei stehender Kamin auf der Terrasse eines Wohnhauses. Kaminkonstruktion aus Beton, zwischen Stütze und Schornstein gespannt; Feuerraum mit 35 mm dicken Schamotteplatten ausgekleidet, die mit starken Schrauben am Beton befestigt werden. (Haus Z, Karlsruhe, entworfen von Reinhard Gieselmann.)

53

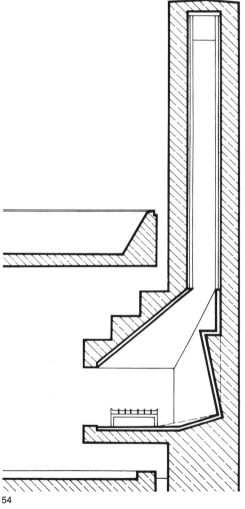

54

55, 56. Combination fireplace with fireboxes on a terrace and in a living room. Fireplace construction of concrete; fireboxes lined with fireclay bricks. The hearth of the interior fireplace has been extended to form a U-shaped bench which integrates the fireplace aesthetically and functionally into the room. (Hengstenberg House, Esslingen, designed by Werner Luz.)

55, 56. Kombinationskamin mit Feuerstellen an einer Terrasse und in einem Wohnraum. Kaminkonstruktion aus Beton; Feuerräume mit Schamottesteinen ausgekleidet. Der Boden des Innenkamins ist zu einer U-förmigen Sitzbank erweitert, die den Kamin formal und funktional in das Raumgeschehen integriert. (Haus Hengstenberg, Esslingen, entworfen von Werner Luz.)

55

56

57, 58. Freestanding fireplace as room-dividing element in a living room. Fireplace construction in natural-stone masonry; firebox and chimney lined with firebricks. The fireplace has an ash-removal device with a down-pipe which extends to the air space under the building. A glass pane mounted in a metal frame serves as spark guard. (Seidler House, Killara, Australia, designed by Harry Seidler & Associates.)

57, 58. Frei stehender, als Raumgliederungselement fungierender Kamin in einem Wohnraum. Kaminkonstruktion in Natursteinmauerwerk; Feuerraum und Schornstein mit feuerfesten Ziegeln ausgekleidet. Der Kamin verfügt über eine Aschenfallkonstruktion mit einem bis in den Luftraum unter dem Gebäude reichenden Fallrohr. Als Funkenschutz dient eine mit einem Metallrahmen gefaßte Glasscheibe. (Seidler House, Killara, Australien, entworfen von Harry Seidler & Associates.)

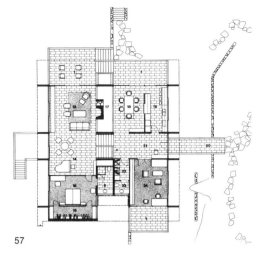

57

58

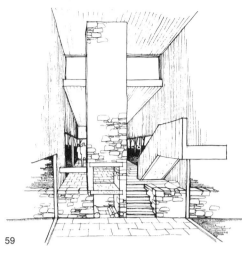

59

59–61. Freestanding fireplace functioning as room-dividing element between a living room and adjoining kitchen area. Fireplace block of concrete, faced with natural stone; firebox of firebricks; smoke flue of terra cotta. The fireplace opens out onto the living room as well as to the kitchen. A firewood niche ist situated under the fireplace opening on the kitchen side. On the living-room side, the fire area can be closed by means of a metal screen. (Wirth House, Westchester County, New York, designed by Alfredo De Vido.)

59–61. Frei stehender, als Raumgliederungselement fungierender Kamin zwischen einem Wohnraum und dem diesem zugeordneten Küchenbereich. Kaminblock aus Beton, verkleidet mit Naturstein; Feuerraum aus feuerfesten Ziegeln; Rauchrohr aus Terrakotta. Der Kamin öffnet sich sowohl zum Wohnraum als auch zur Küche. Auf der Küchenseite befindet sich unter der Feueröffnung eine Holzlege. Auf der Wohnraumseite kann der Feuerraum durch einen Metallvorhang verschlossen werden. (Wirth House, Westchester County, New York, entworfen von Alfredo De Vido.)

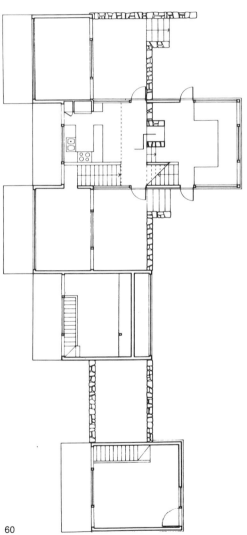

60

61

62. Fireplace forming a wall by itself in a living room. Wall in natural-stone masonry; firebox walls lined with firebricks; hearth as natural stone slab. The fireplace is fitted with supply-air ducts and ash-removal device with ash box in the basement. (Becker Residence, East Hampton, New York, designed by Norman Jaffe.)

62. Eine Wand bildender Kamin in einem Wohnraum. Wand in Natursteinmauerwerk; Feuerraumwände mit feuerfesten Ziegeln ausgekleidet; Feuertisch als Natursteinplatte. Der Kamin ist mit Zuluftkanälen und einer Aschenfallkonstruktion mit Aschenbehälter im Untergeschoß ausgestattet. (Becker Residence, East Hampton, New York, entworfen von Norman Jaffe.)

62

63, 64. Fireplace incorporated in the exterior wall in a living room. Fireplace construction in natural-stone masonry. This fireplace, like the one shown previously, is also fitted with supply-air ducts and an ash-removal device. Metal curtains serve as spark guard. (Perlbinder Residence, Sagaponnack, New York, designed by Norman Jaffe.)

63, 64. In die Außenwand eingebundener Kamin in einem Wohnraum. Kaminkonstruktion in Natursteinmauerwerk. Wie der vorher gezeigte Kamin ist auch dieser mit Zuluftkanälen und einer Aschenfallkonstruktion ausgestattet. Als Funkenschutz dienen Metallvorhänge. (Perlbinder Residence, Sagaponnack, New York, entworfen von Norman Jaffe.)

63

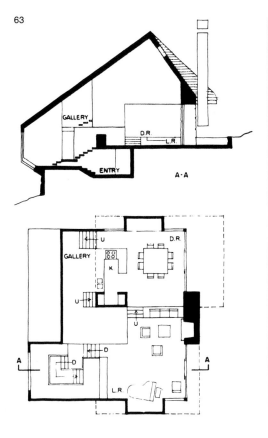

64

65–67. Freestanding combination fireplace with fireboxes in a living room (above) and in a swimming-pool area (below). Fireplace construction in brick masonry, whitewashed, with fireboxes of firebricks. The upper firebox opens to three sides; the lower one has a single opening whose bottom edge lies 1,27 m above the floor, since the fireplace here has been combined with a bar. (Villa in Randers, Denmark, designed by Nils Primdahl & Erich Weitling.)

65–67. Frei stehender Kombinationskamin mit Feuerstellen in einem Wohnraum (oben) und einer Schwimmhalle (unten). Kaminkonstruktion in Ziegelmauerwerk, weiß geschlämmt, mit Feuerräumen aus feuerfesten Steinen. Der obere Feuerraum öffnet sich nach drei Seiten; der untere hat nur eine Feueröffnung, deren Unterkante 1,27 m über dem Fußboden liegt, da der Kamin hier mit einer Bar zusammengeschlossen wurde. (Villa in Randers, Dänemark, entworfen von Nils Primdahl & Erich Weitling.)

66

65

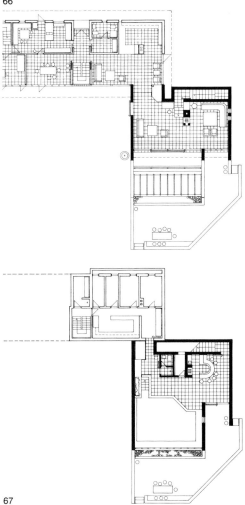

67

68, 69. Freestanding combination fireplace with fireboxes in two living rooms and in the bedroom directly above. Fireplace block in brick masonry with fireboxes of firebricks. The fireplace merits special attention inasmuch as here, a fireplace block not only has three fireboxes, but in addition serves as the nucleus of a circular staircase. (Hale Matthews Residence, East Hampton, New York, designed by Alfredo De Vido.)

68, 69. Frei stehender Kombinationskamin mit Feuerstellen in zwei Wohnräumen und dem darüberliegenden Schlafraum. Kaminblock in Ziegelmauerwerk mit Feuerräumen aus feuerfesten Steinen. Der Kamin verdient insofern besondere Aufmerksamkeit, als hier ein Kaminblock nicht nur drei Feuerstellen zählt, sondern zusätzlich als Kern einer umlaufenden Treppe dient. (Hale Matthews Residence, East Hampton, New York, entworfen von Alfredo De Vido.)

68

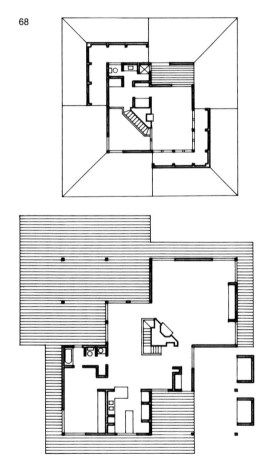

69

70. Freestanding prefabricated fireplace for erection out of doors (model "Mexico" from the company Richard Le Droff, Evry, France). Base of beige-coloured, coarse-grained fossil stone; covering of narrower, brown-red watered, or broader, ochre-yellow watered clinker quarter-bricks. The supplementary elements, adapted to the base, make it possible to extend the fireplace as outdoor seating accommodation. The accessories supplied include a gridiron, two spit holders, two holders for several small spits, two pokers as well as a battery-operated motor spit.

70. Frei stehender Fertigkamin zur Aufstellung im Freien (Modell ,,Mexiko" der Firma Richard Le Droff, Evry, Frankreich). Sockel aus beigefarbenem grobkörnigem Fossilienstein; Abdeckung aus schmaleren braunrot geflammten oder breiteren ockergelb geflammten Klinkerriemchen. Dem Sockel angepaßte Ergänzungselemente erlauben es, den Kamin zu regelrechten Freisitzen zu erweitern. Als Zubehör werden neben einem Grillrost zwei Spießhalter, zwei Halter für mehrere Spießchen, zwei Herdhaken sowie ein batteriebetriebener Motorspieß geliefert.

70

71

72

73. Freestanding fireplace in a living room. Fireplace construction in brick masonry, whitewashed, with firebox of firebricks; cantilever slab beneath the hearth of concrete. (Lorenzen House, Søholmen, Denmark, designed by Lars Børjeson.)

73. Frei stehender Kamin an einer Terrasse. Kaminkonstruktion in Ziegelmauerwerk, weiß gestrichen, mit Feuerraum aus feuerfesten Steinen; Kragplatte unter dem Feuertisch aus Beton. (Haus Lorenzen, Søholmen, Dänemark, entworfen von Lars Børjeson.)

73

71, 72. Freestanding fireplace on a terrace. Fireplace construction in sand-lime brickwork with firebox walls of fireclay bricks; chimney of prefabricated fireclay elements; projecting hearth slab of concrete. A recess at the back of the fireplace serves as firewood niche. (Single-family house in Bogenhausen, Munich, designed by Hans H. Rost.)

71, 72. Frei stehender Kamin an einer Terrasse. Kaminkonstruktion in Kalksandsteinmauerwerk mit Feuerraumwänden aus Schamottesteinen; Schornstein aus Schamotte-Fertigteilen; herausgezogener Feuertisch aus Beton. In der Rückseite des Kamins befindet sich eine als Holzlege nutzbare Aussparung. (Einfamilienhaus in München-Bogenhausen, entworfen von Hans H. Rost.)

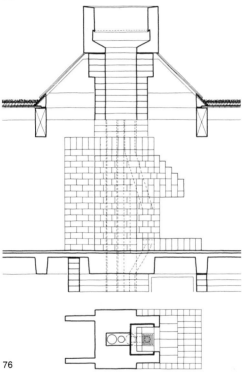

74–77. Freestanding fireplace in a living room. Fireplace construction in sand-lime brickwork with firebox of fireclay bricks; smoke discharge by steel-plate pipe. The fireplace is equipped with an ash-removal device. Apart from the smoke flue of the fireplace, the chimney block accommodates the smoke flue of the central heating as well as an air-vent pipe. A coat rack hangs between the two walls at the back of the fireplace. (Combined dwelling house and office in Karlsruhe, designed by Heinz Mohl.)

74–77. Frei stehender Kamin in einem Wohnraum. Kaminkonstruktion in Kalksandsteinmauerwerk mit Feuerraum aus Schamottesteinen; Rauchabführung als Stahlblechrohr. Der Kamin ist mit einer Aschenfallkonstruktion ausgerüstet. Der Schornsteinblock nimmt neben dem Rauchrohr des Kamins das Rauchrohr der Zentralheizung sowie ein Entlüftungsrohr auf. Zwischen den beiden rückwärtigen Mauerscheiben befindet sich eine Garderobe. (Wohn- und Geschäftshaus in Karlsruhe, entworfen von Heinz Mohl.)

77

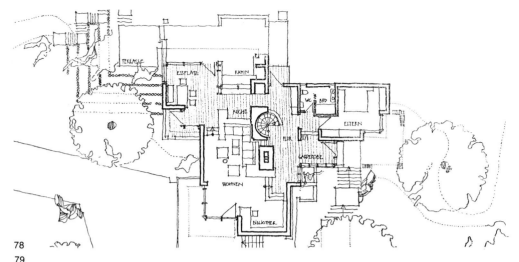

78

79

78, 79. Fireplace incorporated in an exterior wall on a terrace. Fireplace construction in sand-lime brickwork, whitewashed. The fireplace is combined with a bench, situated in a sheltered spot, and a firewood niche. (Residence of an art dealer in Dreieichenhain near Frankfurt, designed by Jochem Jourdan.)

78, 79. In eine Außenwand eingebundener Kamin an einer Terrasse. Kaminkonstruktion in Kalksandsteinmauerwerk, weiß gestrichen. Der Kamin ist mit einer windgeschützt gelegenen Sitzbank und einer Holzlege kombiniert. (Wohnhaus eines Kunsthändlers in Dreieichenhain bei Frankfurt am Main, entworfen von Jochem Jourdan.)

80, 81. Combination fireplace incorporated in an exterior wall with two fireboxes on a terrace and one firebox in a living room. Fireplace construction in brick masonry, whitewashed, with fireboxes of firebricks. The middle fire space has been constructed as a cooking stove; the fire burns in a closed firebox under an iron plate with two cooking rings. (Country house in Sandbjerg, Denmark, designed by Bertel Udsen.)

80, 81. In eine Außenwand eingebundener Kombinationskamin mit zwei Feuerstellen an einer Terrasse und einer Feuerstelle in einem Wohnraum. Kaminkonstruktion in Ziegelmauerwerk, weiß gestrichen, mit Feuerräumen aus feuerfesten Steinen. Der mittlere Feuerplatz ist als Herd ausgebildet; das Feuer brennt in einem geschlossenen Feuerraum unter einer mit zwei Herdringen ausgestatteten Eisenplatte. (Landhaus in Sandbjerg, Dänemark, entworfen von Bertel Udsen.)

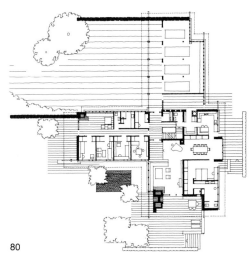

80

81

82

83

82. Fireplace incorporated in an exterior wall in a living room (to the right, dining area, to the left, seating area). Fireplace construction in brick masonry with firebox of firebricks. In order to eliminate the danger of flying sparks, a metal-mesh screen was fitted into the firebox which restricts the burning space to the inner corner. (Mogensen House, Gentofte, Denmark, designed by Børge Mogensen and Erling Zeuthen Nielsen.)

83. Fireplace incorporated in an exterior wall in a living room. Fireplace construction in brick masonry; smoke hood of metal; free part of the smoke flue of stainless steel, thermally insulated. The firebox receives a direct supply of air from the exterior. Two loudspeakers are built into the brickwork fronts on either side of the fireplace; the continuous surface which runs along above the hearth, approximately at table level, serves as spacious shelf area. (Thurlow House, Cambridge, England, designed by David Thurlow.)

84. Fireplace incorporated in a medium-high partition wall in a living room. Fireplace construction in brick masonry; continuous base and firebox frame of polished slate. An ash box located in the base may be lifted out for emptying. The firebox is directly linked with the outside air by means of supply-air ducts. (Robert Welch House, Stratford-upon-Avon, England, designed by Patrick Guest.)

82. In eine Außenwand eingebundener Kamin in einem Wohnraum (rechts Eßplatz, links Sitzplatz). Kaminkonstruktion in Ziegelmauerwerk mit Feuerraum aus feuerfesten Steinen. Um der Gefahr des Funkenflugs zu begegnen, wurde im Feuerraum ein Metallgitter angebracht, das den Brennplatz auf die innere Ecke begrenzt. (Haus Mogensen, Gentofte, Dänemark, entworfen von Børge Mogensen und Erling Zeuthen Nielsen.)

83. In eine Außenwand eingebundener Kamin in einem Wohnraum. Kaminkonstruktion in Ziegelmauerwerk; Rauchschürze aus Metall; freier Teil des Rauchrohrs aus Edelstahl, wärmegedämmt. Der Feuerraum erhält direkte Zuluft von außen. In die Felder neben dem Kamin sind zwei Lautsprecher eingelassen, die etwa auf Tischhöhe liegende durchlaufende Fläche dient als geräumige Ablage. (Thurlow House, Cambridge, England, entworfen von David Thurlow.)

84. In eine halbhohe Trennwand eingebundener Kamin in einem Wohnraum. Kaminkonstruktion in Ziegelmauerwerk; durchlaufender Sockel und Feuerraumeinfassung aus poliertem Schiefer. Im Sockel befindet sich ein nach oben zu entleerender Aschenbehälter. Der Feuerraum ist mit Zuluftkanälen direkt an die Außenluft angeschlossen. (Robert Welch House, Stratford-upon-Avon, England, entworfen von Patrick Guest.)

85. Wall-incorporated fireplace in a living room. Fireplace construction in brick masonry with firebox of firebricks. The damper is regulated with a rod which extends down into the firebox. (Villa Heilmann, Holte, Denmark, designed by Bertel Udsen.)

85. In eine Wand eingebundener Kamin in einem Wohnraum. Kaminkonstruktion in Ziegelmauerwerk mit Feuerraum aus feuerfesten Steinen. Die Rauchklappe wird mit einem in den Feuerraum herunterreichenden Gestänge betätigt. (Villa Heilmann, Holte, Dänemark, entworfen von Bertel Udsen.)

86. Wall-incorporated fireplace in a living room. Fireplace construction in brick masonry. The hearth has been extended to form a bench with plant alcove. A removable screen serves as spark guard. (Jürgensen House, Lyngby, Denmark, designed by Carla and Axel Jürgensen.)

86. In eine Wand eingebundener Kamin in einem Wohnraum. Kaminkonstruktion in Ziegelmauerwerk. Der Kaminboden ist zu einem breiten Sockel mit Pflanzgrube erweitert. Gegen Funkenflug schützt ein wegnehmbares Gitter. (Haus Jürgensen, Lyngby, Dänemark, entworfen von Carla und Axel Jürgensen.)

87

86

87. Wall-incorporated fireplace in a living room. Fireplace construction in brick masonry, whitewashed, with firebox of firebricks. An additional stove with separate chimney is attached to the fireplace block. (Summer house in Rørvig, Denmark, designed by Bertel Udsen.)

87. In eine Wand eingebundener Kamin in einem Wohnraum. Kaminkonstruktion in Ziegelmauerwerk, weiß geschlämmt, mit Feuerraum aus feuerfesten Steinen. An den Kaminblock ist ein zusätzlicher Ofen mit eigenem Schornstein angeschlossen. (Sommerhaus in Rørvig, Dänemark, entworfen von Bertel Udsen.)

88. Fireplace block in a living room. Fireplace construction in brick masonry with firebox of firebricks. As protection against flying sparks, the fireplace has a safety area in front of the hearth consisting of clinkers set flush with the floor. (Vacation house in Liseleje, Denmark, designed by Bertel Udsen.)

88. Einen Block bildender Kamin in einem Wohnraum. Kaminkonstruktion in Ziegelmauerwerk mit Feuerraum aus feuerfesten Steinen. Zum Schutz gegen Funkenflug ist dem Kamin ein Sicherheitsstreifen aus bodenbündig verlegten Ziegelsteinen vorgelagert. (Ferienhaus in Liseleje, Dänemark, entworfen von Bertel Udsen.)

88

89

89. Combination fireplace incorporated in a wall with fireboxes in a living room (above; see photograph) and in a small fireplace room (below; not illustrated). Fireplace construction in brick masonry with fireboxes of firebricks. Apart from a firewood niche located at the side (not visible in the photograph), the upper fireplace has a projecting hearth as well as a broad brickwork shelf. (Villa Thøgersen, Vedbaek, Denmark, designed by Bertel Udsen.)

89. In eine Wand eingebundener Kombinationskamin mit Feuerstellen in einem Wohnraum (oben; siehe Abbildung) und in einer Kaminstube (unten; nicht abgebildet). Kaminkonstruktion in Ziegelmauerwerk mit Feuerräumen aus feuerfesten Steinen. Neben einer seitlich angeordneten Holzlege (auf der Abbildung nicht sichtbar) hat der obere Kamin einen weit vorgezogenen Feuertisch sowie eine breite Ablagebank. (Villa Thøgersen, Vedbaek, Dänemark, entworfen von Bertel Udsen.)

90, 91. Wall-incorporated fireplace in a living room. Fireplace construction in brick masonry with firebox of firebricks. Firewood niche and firebox are uniform in appearance. The hearth has been extended at the front to form a spacious shelf. (Villa Holt, Holte, Denmark, designed by Bertel Udsen.)

90, 91. In eine Wand eingebundener Kamin in einem Wohnraum. Kaminkonstruktion in Ziegelmauerwerk mit Feuerraum aus feuerfesten Steinen. Feuerraum und Holzlege sind formal zusammengefaßt, der Feuertisch ist nach vorn zu einer geräumigen Ablage erweitert. (Villa Holt, Holte, Dänemark, entworfen von Bertel Udsen.)

90

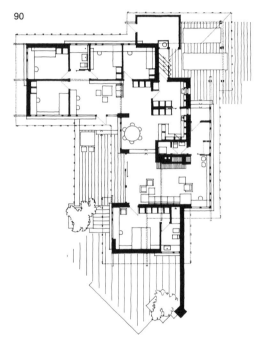

91

92

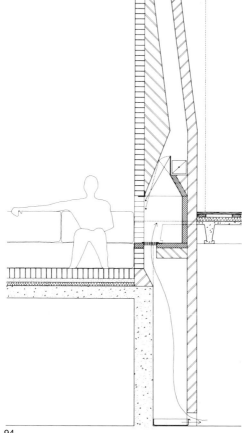

93

94

90

92–94. Wall-incorporated fireplace in front of a sunken seating area in a living room. Wall facing in brick masonry, whitewashed; firebox of firebricks. The fireplace is equipped with a device for ash removal which is directly supplied with air; the ash pit opens into the garage. The fire-irons hang on a black iron plate. (House in Isles-les-Villenois, France, designed by Michel Mortier.)

92–94. In eine Wand eingebundener Kamin vor einer Sitzgrube in einem Wohnraum. Wandverkleidung in Ziegelmauerwerk, weiß gestrichen; Feuerraum aus feuerfesten Steinen. Der Kamin ist mit einer Aschenfallkonstruktion mit gleichzeitiger direkter Luftzuführung ausgestattet; der Aschenschacht mündet in der Garage. Das Feuerbesteck hängt auf einer schwarzen Eisenplatte. (Haus in Isles-les-Villenois, Frankreich, entworfen von Michel Mortier.)

95, 96. Wall-incorporated fireplace in front of a sunken seating area in a living room. Wall in brick masonry with firebox of firebricks. The fireplace is equipped with a device for ash removal; the pit opens into the basement. A removable metal-mesh curtain serves as spark guard. (Villa Graf, Céligny, Switzerland, designed by Annen, Siebold, Siegle.)

95, 96. In eine Wand eingebundener Kamin vor einer Sitzgrube in einem Wohnraum. Wand in Ziegelmauerwerk mit Feuerraum aus feuerfesten Steinen. Der Kamin ist mit einer Aschenfallkonstruktion ausgestattet, der Schacht mündet im Untergeschoß. Als Funkenschutz dient ein wegnehmbares Metallgewebe. (Villa Graf, Céligny, Schweiz, entworfen von Annen, Siebold, Siegle.)

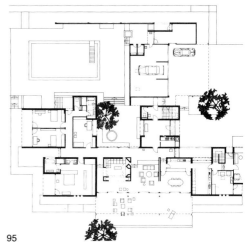

95

96

97

97–99. Two freestanding fireplaces in a living and dining-room. Fireplace construction in brickwork, plastered. The hearth projects slightly to protect the plaster. The two fireplaces subdivide the some 16 m long room and help to screen off the entrance area. (Casa Sert, Punta Martinet, Spain, designed by Josep Lluis Sert.)

97–99. Zwei frei stehende Kamine in einem Wohn- und Speiseraum. Kaminkonstruktion in Mauerwerk, verputzt. Der Feuertisch ist zum Schutz des Putzes etwas vorgezogen. Durch die beiden Kamine wird der etwa 16 m lange Raum gegliedert und der Zugangsbereich ein wenig abgeschirmt. (Casa Sert, Punta Martinet, Spanien, entworfen von Josep Lluis Sert.)

98

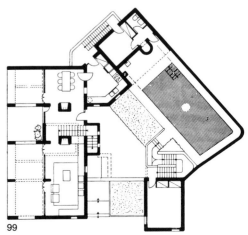

99

100–102. Combination fireplace incorporated in a parapet with a firebox in a family room (below) and in a living room (above). Fireplace structure in brickwork, plastered, with fireboxes of firebricks; smoke flues of terra cotta with a mantle of asbestos cement. The lintels above the fireplace openings consist of steel angles whose horizontal legs jut out 4 cm over the plaster area to reduce contamination through smoke emission. (Frisch Residence, Ashley Falls, Massachusetts, designed by Julian and Barbara Neski.)

100–102. In eine Brüstung eingebundener Kombinationskamin mit einer Feuerstelle in einem Familienraum (unten) und einem Wohnraum (oben). Kaminkörper in Mauerwerk, verputzt, mit Feuerräumen aus feuerfesten Steinen; Rauchrohre aus Terrakotta mit einem Mantel aus Astbestzement. Die Stürze über den Feueröffnungen bestehen aus Stahlwinkeln, deren liegende Schenkel knapp 4 cm über die Putzfläche hinausragen, um Verschmutzung durch Rauchaustritt zu vermindern. (Frisch Residence, Ashley Falls, Massachusetts, entworfen von Julian und Barbara Neski.)

101

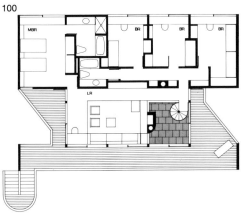

100

102

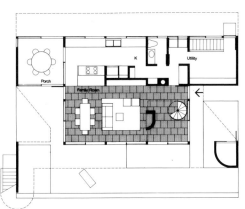

103

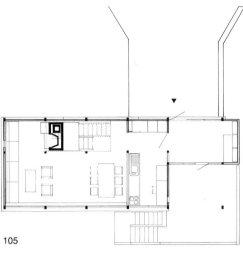

105

104

103–105. Fireplace combined with a staircase standing free in front of a wall in a living room. Fireplace structure in brickwork, plastered; firebox as prefabricated fireclay element (Cheminée Honegger, Zurich); bench in front of the firebox with a top covering of gray cement. The fireplace receives supply air from the basement; the air outlet is located on the front side of the bench in front of the firebox. The chimney for the central heating is incorporated in the fireplace block. (Vacation house Wechsler, Wasserwendi-Hasliberg, Switzerland, designed by Hannes Ineichen.)

103–105. Frei vor einer Wand stehender, mit einer Treppe kombinierter Kamin in einem Wohnraum. Kaminkörper in Mauerwerk, verputzt; Feuerraum als Schamotte-Fertigteil (Cheminée Honegger, Zürich); Sockel vor dem Feuerraum auf der Oberseite mit grauem Zement überzogen. Der Kamin erhält Zuluft aus dem Keller; der Luftaustritt befindet sich auf der Stirnseite des Sockels vor dem Feuerraum. In den Kaminblock einbezogen ist der Schornstein für die Zentralheizung. (Ferienhaus Wechsler, Wasserwendi-Hasliberg, Schweiz, entworfen von Hannes Ineichen.)

106

107

106, 107. Freestanding fireplace in a living room with a firebox in the seating area (fig. 106) and an elevated grill space in the dining area (fig. 107). Fireplace construction in brickwork, plastered, with fireboxes and safety areas of fireclay bricks; shelf and seating areas covered with glazed white clinker slabs. The fireplace receives a direct supply of fresh air through ducts. The fire space has an ash box, the grill space an ash drawer. (Vacation house Dr. Wydler, Klosters, Switzerland, designed by Hans and Marguerite Dreher.)

106, 107. Frei stehender Kamin in einem Wohnraum mit einem Fensterplatz am Sitzbereich (Abb. 106) und einem hochgelegenen Grillplatz am Eßbereich (Abb. 107). Kaminkonstruktion in Mauerwerk aus Leichtbetonsteinen, verputzt, mit Feuerräumen und Sicherheitsstreifen aus Schamottesteinen; Abdeckung der Ablage- und Sitzflächen aus glasierten weißen Klinkerplatten. Der Kamin ist mit einer direkten Frischluftzuführung durch Kanäle ausgestattet. Der Feuerplatz hat einen Aschenbehälter, der Grillplatz eine Aschenschublade. (Ferienhaus Dr. Wydler, Klosters, Schweiz, entworfen von Hans und Marguerite Dreher.)

108, 109. Freestanding fireplace in front of a fixed seating area in a fireplace room. Fireplace construction in brick masonry, faced with plaster at the front and with gypsum sheets at the rear, with fireboxes of firebricks; base in front of the firebox covered with natural-stone slabs; chimney lining of firebrick panels. The fireplace is equipped with a device for ash removal which opens into the basement. A two-part metal-mesh screen serves as spark guard. The chimney of the central heating is incorporated in the chimney block. (Koizim Residence, Westport, Connecticut, designed by Charles W. Moore and MLTW/Turnbull Associates.)

108, 109. Frei stehender Kamin vor einem fest-eingebauten Sitzplatz in einem Kaminraum. Kaminkonstruktion in Ziegelmauerwerk, auf der Vorderseite verputzt und auf der Rückseite mit Gipsplatten verkleidet, mit Feuerraum aus feuerfesten Steinen; Sockel vor dem Feuerraum mit Natursteinplatten belegt; Schornsteinauskleidung aus feuerfesten Ziegelplatten. Der Kamin ist mit einer im Keller mündenden Aschenfallkonstruktion ausgestattet. Als Funkenschutz dient ein zweiteiliges Metallgitter. In den Kaminblock einbezogen ist der Schornstein der Zentralheizung. (Koizim Residence, Westport, Connecticut, entworfen von Charles W. Moore und MLTW/Turnbull Associates.)

108

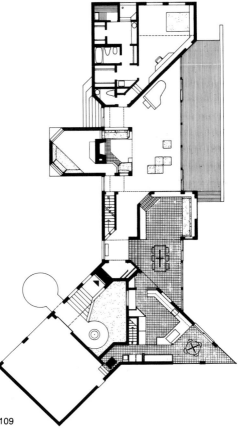

109

110. Wall-incorporated fireplace in the hall of an ecclesiastical centre. Base and side walls of concrete, plastered; hood as wire lath and plaster shell; hearth as sheet of iron (with ash grate in front); firebox walls lined with fireclay slabs; neck of sheet metal; chimney of prefabricated fireclay elements (Plewa tubes). An ash drawer, which pulls out at the front, is situated under the hearth. A spark guard is not included. (Haus St. Ulrich – Academy and Pastoral Centre of the Diocese of Augsburg–, Augsburg, designed by Alexander Freiherr von Branca.)

110. In eine Wand eingebundener Kamin in der Halle eines kirchlichen Zentrums. Sockel und Seitenwände aus Beton, verputzt; Haube als Drahtputzschale; Feuertisch als Eisenplatte (davor Aschenfallrost); Feuerraumwände mit Schamotteplatten ausgekleidet; Rauchhals aus Blech; Schornstein aus Schamotte-Fertigteilen (Plewa-Rohre). Unter der Feuerstelle befindet sich ein nach vorn herausziehbarer Aschenkasten. Ein Funkenschutz ist nicht vorhanden. (Haus St. Ulrich – Akademie und Seelsorgezentrum der Diözese Augsburg –, Augsburg, entworfen von Alexander Freiherr von Branca.)

110

111, 112. Fireplace incorporated in an exterior wall in a two-storey-high living room. Fireplace construction in concrete-block masonry, plastered, with fireboxes of firebricks. As protection against flying sparks, a safety area of stone slabs has been sunk into the wood floor in front of the fireplace. Fireplace structure and chimney are staggered relatively to each other at an angle of 45°, thus complying with the structural composition of the room. (Benenson Residence, Hawley, Pennsylvania, designed by Mayers & Schiff.)

111, 112. In eine Außenwand eingebundener Kamin in einem zwei Geschoß hohen Wohnraum. Kaminkonstruktion in Betonsteinmauerwerk, verputzt, mit Feuerraum aus feuerfesten Ziegeln. Zum Schutz gegen Funkenflug befindet sich vor dem Kamin ein bündig in den Holzfußboden eingelassener Streifen aus Steinplatten. Kaminkörper und Schornstein sind um 45° gegeneinander verdreht und nehmen damit Bezug auf den kompositorischen Aufbau des Raumes. (Benenson Residence, Hawley, Pennsylvania, entworfen von Mayers & Schiff.)

111

112

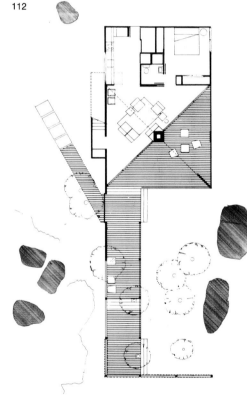

113, 114. Combination fireplace incorporated in an exterior wall with fireboxes in a family room (below) and in a living room (above). Fireplace construction in brickwork, plastered, fireboxes lined with soapstone, chimneys with terra cotta. The soapstone slabs project slightly to protect the plaster. Since the ceiling between the ground and upper floor is a wood-beam construction covered with deal boards, a cantilever concrete slab with a covering of stone slabs has been arranged in front of the upper fireplace. (Kaplan Residence, New York, designed by Julian and Barbara Neski.)

113, 114. In eine Außenwand eingebundener Kombinationskamin mit Feuerstellen in einem Familienraum (unten) und einem Wohnraum (oben). Kaminkonstruktion in Mauerwerk, verputzt; Feuerräume mit Speckstein, Schornsteine mit Terrakotta ausgekleidet. Die Specksteinplatten sind zum Schutz des Putzes etwas vorgezogen. Da die Decke zwischen Erd- und Obergeschoß eine mit Dielen belegte Holzbalkenkonstruktion ist, wurde vor dem oberen Kamin eine Kragplatte aus Beton angeordnet und diese mit Steinplatten belegt. (Kaplan Residence, East Hampton, New York, entworfen von Julian und Barbara Neski.)

113

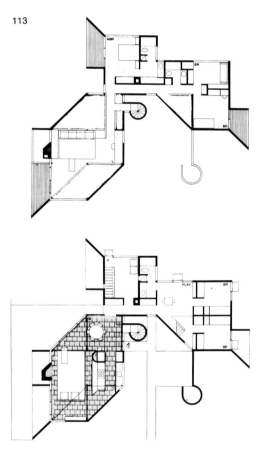

114

115. Combination fireplace incorporated in an exterior wall with firebox in a two-storey-high living room (above) and in a playroom (below; not shown here). Fireplace construction in brick masonry, plastered, with fireboxes of firebricks. Chimneys lined with firebrick slabs. As protection against flying sparks, the fireboxes can be closed with mesh curtains. Above the fireplace block, the chimney shaft runs free in front of the glass wall. (Victor Sklar Residence, Westchester County, New York, designed by Christopher H. L. Owen.)

115. In eine Außenwand eingebundener Kombinationskamin mit Feuerstelle in einem zwei Geschoß hohen Wohnraum (oben) und einem Spielraum (unten; hier nicht gezeigt). Kaminkonstruktion in Ziegelmauerwerk, verputzt, mit Feuerräumen aus feuerfesten Steinen; Schornsteine mit Ziegelplatten ausgekleidet. Zum Schutz gegen Funkenflug können die Feuerräume mit Metallvorhängen verschlossen werden. Ab der halben Höhe der Wohnhalle verläuft der Schornsteinschaft frei vor der Glaswand. (Victor Sklar Residence, Westchester County, New York, entworfen von Christopher H. L. Owen.)

115

116

116. Fireplace incorporated in an exterior wall in a living room. Hearth of clinker slabs; neck hood of steel plate; hood facing as wire lath and plaster shell; chimney in hard-brick masonry. To increase the heat reflection, three iron plates have been fitted to the back wall of the firebox. The fireplace is equipped with a device for ash removal, over which air is simultaneously conveyed to the fire. (Formerly, Gieselmann House, Karlsruhe, designed by Reinhard Gieselmann.)

116. In eine Außenwand eingebundener Kamin in einem Wohnraum. Feuertisch aus Klinkerplatten; Rauchhalshaube aus Stahlblech; Haubenverkleidung als Drahtputzschale; Schornstein in Hartbrandziegelmauerwerk. Zur Erhöhung der Wärmereflexion sind an der Feuerraumrückwand drei Eisenplatten angebracht. Der Kamin ist mit einer Aschenfallkonstruktion, über die zugleich Luft zugeführt wird, ausgestattet. (Ehemaliges Haus Gieselmann, Karlsruhe, entworfen von Reinhard Gieselmann.)

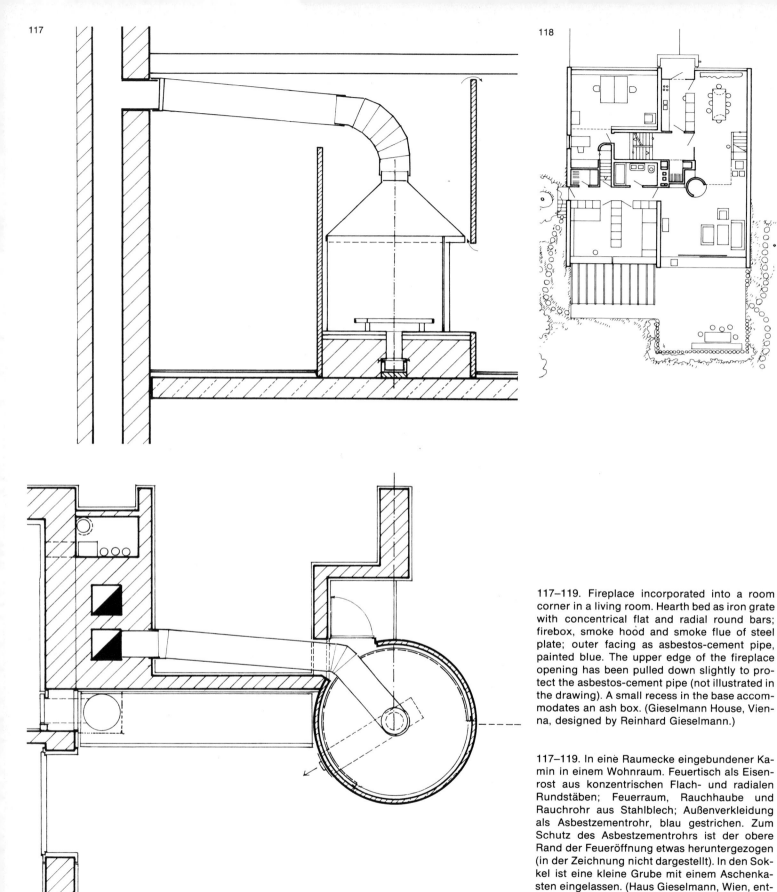

117

118

117–119. Fireplace incorporated into a room corner in a living room. Hearth bed as iron grate with concentrical flat and radial round bars; firebox, smoke hood and smoke flue of steel plate; outer facing as asbestos-cement pipe, painted blue. The upper edge of the fireplace opening has been pulled down slightly to protect the asbestos-cement pipe (not illustrated in the drawing). A small recess in the base accommodates an ash box. (Gieselmann House, Vienna, designed by Reinhard Gieselmann.)

117–119. In eine Raumecke eingebundener Kamin in einem Wohnraum. Feuertisch als Eisenrost aus konzentrischen Flach- und radialen Rundstäben; Feuerraum, Rauchhaube und Rauchrohr aus Stahlblech; Außenverkleidung als Asbestzementrohr, blau gestrichen. Zum Schutz des Asbestzementrohrs ist der obere Rand der Feueröffnung etwas heruntergezogen (in der Zeichnung nicht dargestellt). In den Sokkel ist eine kleine Grube mit einem Aschenkasten eingelassen. (Haus Gieselmann, Wien, entworfen von Reinhard Gieselmann.)

120. Fireplace standing free in front of a light partition wall in a living room. Rear part in natural-stone masonry; hearth and hood of black-enamelled steel plate. (Goodyear House, designed by John M. Johansen.)

120. Frei vor einer leichten Trennwand stehender Kamin in einem Wohnraum. Rückwärtiger Teil in Natursteinmauerwerk; Feuertisch und Haube aus Stahlblech, schwarz lackiert. (Goodyear House, entworfen von John M. Johansen.)

121

122

121, 122. Freestanding fireplace combined with a gallery in a living room. Chimney block and side wall in sand-lime brickwork with sides adjacent to the firebox lined with fireclay; hood of black-enamelled steel plate, thermally insulated. The fire is directly linked with the outside air by means of air ducts. Since the carpeting on the one side runs right up to the fireplace, the slate flooring on the other side has been drawn round and extended to form a small platform in front of the hearth. As additional protection against flying sparks, a fine-meshed screen may be placed in front of the fire. (Single-family house in Bogenhausen, Munich, designed by Hans H. Rost.)

121, 122. Frei stehender, mit einer Galerie verbundener Kamin in einem Wohnraum. Schornsteinblock und Seitenwange in Kalksandsteinmauerwerk mit feuerseitiger Schamotteauskleidung; Haube aus Stahlblech, wärmegedämmt und schwarz lackiert. Der Kamin ist mit Zuluftkanälen direkt an die Außenluft angeschlossen. Da auf der einen Seite des Kamins ein Teppichbelag anschließt, wurde hier der Schieferboden der anderen Seite herumgezogen und zu einem kleinen Podest erweitert. Zusätzlich kann als Funkenschutz ein Gestell mit Metallgewebe aufgestellt werden. (Einfamilienhaus in München-Bogenhausen, entworfen von Hans H. Rost.)

123

124

123, 124. Wall-incorporated fireplace in a living room. Side walls in hard-burned brick masonry; hood of enamelled steel plate. The floor of clay tiles extends into the fireplace to form the hearth; the fire burns on an iron grate. (Geratewohl House, Steinebach, Germany, designed by Ernst Fischer.)

123, 124. In eine Wand eingebundener Kamin in einem Wohnraum. Seitenwangen in Mauerwerk aus Hartbrandziegeln; Haube aus Stahlblech, lackiert. Der Kaminboden besteht wie der Bodenbelag des ganzen Wohnraums aus Tonplatten; das Feuer brennt auf einem Eisenrost. (Haus Geratewohl, Steinebach, Bayern, entworfen von Ernst Fischer.)

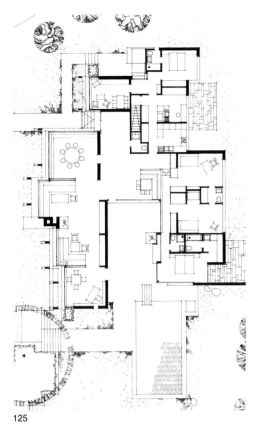

125

126

125–127. Fireplace incorporated in an exterior wall in a living room. Substructure in brick masonry with firebox of fireclay bricks; neck as prefabricated steel-plate element; hood of copper plate. The fireplace has a device for ash removal with ash box in the basement. A glass plate between hood and hearth protects the curtains, which border on the left side of the fireplace, against flying sparks. (Country house Kürsteiner, Greifensee near Zurich, designed by Justus Dahinden.)

125–127. In eine Außenwand eingebundener Kamin in einem Wohnraum. Unterkonstruktion in Ziegelmauerwerk mit Feuerraum aus Schamottesteinen; Rauchhals als Stahlblech-Fertigteil; Haube aus Kupferblech. Der Kamin besitzt eine Aschenfallkonstruktion mit Aschenbehälter im Untergeschoß. Als Funkenschutz gegen die links an den Kamin anschließenden Vorhänge dient eine zwischen Haube und Feuertisch gestellte Glasplatte. (Landhaus Kürsteiner, Greifensee bei Zürich, entworfen von Justus Dahinden.)

128–130. Freestanding fireplace in a living room. Floor zone (hearth and safety area) of natural-stone slabs; fireplace block in natural-stone masonry; firebox walls lined with firebricks; plastered neck; smoke flue in brickwork, inside plastered, outside whitewashed. The fireplace has a device for ash removal with downpipe to the basement. As protection against flying sparks, two-part metal-mesh curtains have been fitted on either side of the fireplace opening. (Ski hut in Thredbo, Australia, designed by Harry Seidler.)

128–130. Frei stehender Kamin in einem Wohnraum. Bodenzone (Feuerfläche und Sicherheitsstreifen) aus Natursteinplatten; Kaminblock in Natursteinmauerwerk; Feuerraumwände mit feuerfesten Steinen ausgekleidet; Rauchhals verputzt; Rauchrohr in Ziegelmauerwerk, innen verputzt, außen geschlämmt. Der Kamin besitzt eine Aschenfallkonstruktion mit Fallrohr zum Untergeschoß. Zum Schutz gegen Funkenflug sind auf beiden Seiten der Feueröffnung zweiteilige Metallvorhänge angebracht. (Skihütte in Thredbo, Australien, entworfen von Harry Seidler.)

128

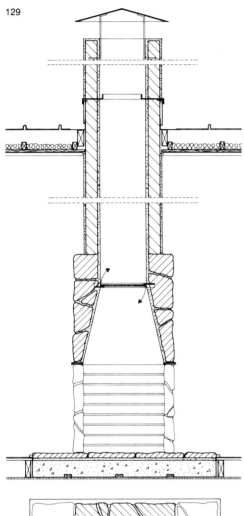

129

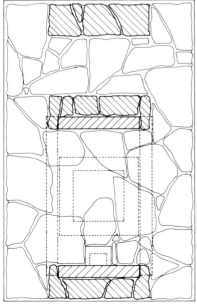

130

131, 132. Freestanding combination fireplace with fireboxes in an upper (fig. 132) and a lower living room. Fireplace block in brick masonry with firebox walls of fireclay bricks; intermediate and marginal components as prefabricated concrete elements. (Hoffmann-Lindenau House, Bad Herrenalb, Germany, designed by Karl-Heinz Götz.)

131, 132. Frei stehender Kombinationskamin mit Feuerstellen in einem oberen (Abb. 132) und einem unteren Wohnraum. Kaminblock in Ziegelmauerwerk mit Feuerraumwänden aus Schamottesteinen; Zwischen- und Randelemente als Beton-Fertigteile. (Haus Hoffmann-Lindenau, Bad Herrenalb, entworfen von Karl-Heinz Götz.)

131

132

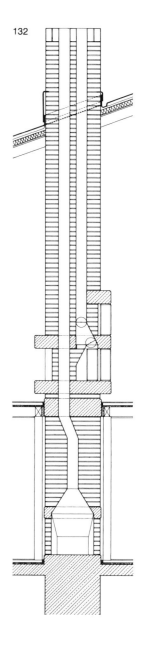

133, 134. Freestanding fireplace with additional grill space on the terrace of a residence. Underframe of concrete with side walls in brick masonry; chimney block in brick masonry; grill and ash box under the grill of steel; shelf behind the grill covered with stoneware tiles. To protect the wooden terrace floor, the hearth slab in front of the fireplace has been constructed in the form of a tub and slightly extended. The chimney block accommodates two additional chimneys for central heating. (Hoffmann-Lindenau House, Bad Herrenalb, Germany, designed by Karl-Heinz Götz.)

133, 134. Frei stehender Kamin mit zusätzlichem Grillplatz auf der Terrasse eines Wohnhauses. Unterteil aus Beton mit seitlichen Wangen in Ziegelmauerwerk; Schornsteinblock in Ziegelmauerwerk; Grillrost und Aschenkasten unter dem Rost aus Stahl; Ablage hinter dem Grill mit Steinzeugfliesen belegt. Zum Schutz des aus Holz bestehenden Terrassenbodens ist der Feuertisch des Kamins als Wanne ausgebildet und etwas vorgezogen. In dem Schornsteinblock sind zusätzlich zwei Schornsteine für Zentralheizungen untergebracht. (Haus Hoffmann-Lindenau, Bad Herrenalb, entworfen von Karl-Heinz Götz.)

134

133

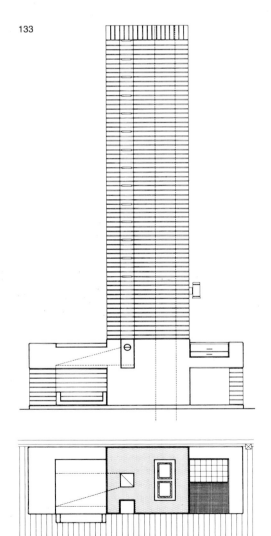

135, 136. Wall-incorporated fireplace in a living room. Fireplace block in sand-lime brickwork, whitewashed; firebox of refractory concrete; forehearth and smoke hood of plain concrete; chimney of prefabricated fireclay elements ("Plewa" pipes). (Single-family house in Kranichstein, Darmstadt, designed by Rolf Poth.)

135, 136. In eine Wand eingebundener Kamin in einem Wohnraum. Kaminblock in Kalksandsteinmauerwerk, weiß geschlämmt; Feuerraum aus feuerfestem Beton; Vorherd und Rauchhaube aus normalem Beton; Schornstein aus Schamotte-Fertigteilen („Plewa"-Rohre). (Einfamilienhaus in Darmstadt-Kranichstein, entworfen von Rolf Poth.)

135

136

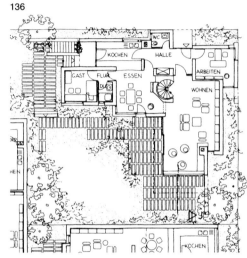

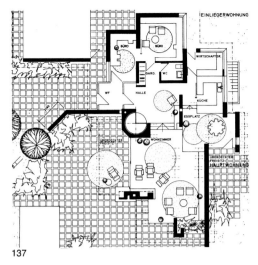

137

138

139

137–139. Combination fireplace with fireboxes on a terrace and in a living room. Fireplace block in brick masonry with firebox of fireclay bricks; forehearth and smoke hood of concrete. (Baumüller House, Kranichstein, Darmstadt, designed by Rolf Poth.)

137–139. Kombinationskamin mit Feuerstellen an einer Terrasse und in einem Wohnraum. Kaminblock in Ziegelmauerwerk mit Feuerraum aus Schamottesteinen; Vorherd und Rauchhaube aus Beton. (Haus Baumüller, Darmstadt-Kranichstein, entworfen von Rolf Poth.)

140–143. Fireplace standing free in front of a wall in a living room. Fireplace structure in sand-lime brickwork with firebox of fireclay bricks; base and smoke hood of painted concrete. The fireplace is equipped with a device for ash removal. In order to integrate the fireplace as far as possible in the room, the base zone was extended to the end wall of the living room. (Poth House, Kranichstein, Darmstadt, designed by Rolf Poth.)

140–143. Frei vor einer Wand stehender Kamin in einem Wohnraum. Kaminkörper in Kalksandsteinmauerwerk mit Feuerraum aus Schamottesteinen; Sockel und Rauchhaube aus Beton, gestrichen. Der Kamin ist mit einer Aschenfallkonstruktion ausgestattet. Um den Kamin soweit wie möglich in den Raum zu integrieren, wurde die Sockelzone bis zur Abschlußwand des Wohnraums weitergeführt. (Haus Poth, Darmstadt-Kranichstein, entworfen von Rolf Poth.)

140

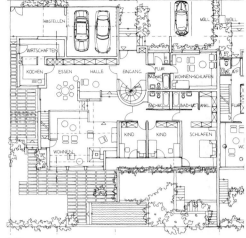

141

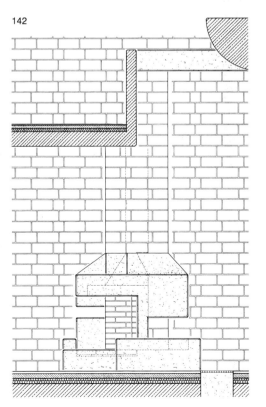

142

143

144

145

144–146. Wall-incorporated fireplace in a living room. Wall in brick masonry with firebox of firebricks; base zone and crossbeam of concrete; shelf surface on the crossbeam of wood. The firebox is directly linked with the outside air through air ducts. The front hearth has been considerably extended as protection against flying sparks. Since the ash pit is open at the front, the removal of ash is a simple task. (Residence in Udine, Italy, designed by Carlo Mangani.)

144–146. In eine Wand eingebundener Kamin in einem Wohnraum. Wand in Ziegelmauerwerk mit Feuerraum aus feuerfesten Steinen; Sockelzone und Querbalken aus Beton; Ablagefläche auf dem Querbalken aus Holz. Der Feuerraum ist durch Kanäle direkt mit der Außenluft verbunden. Zum Schutz gegen Funkenflug wurde der Feuertisch weit vorgezogen. Da die Aschengrube nach vorn offen ist, läßt sich die Asche sehr leicht entfernen. (Wohnhaus in Udine, Italien, entworfen von Carlo Mangani.)

146

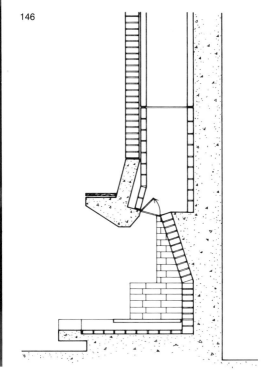

147. Wall-incorporated fireplace in a patio. Wall in brick masonry with firebox of firebricks; lintel above the firebox and firewood niche of concrete. A small bricked sunken seating area helps to integrate the fireplace in its surroundings. (Residence in Udine, Italy, designed by Carlo Mangani.)

147. In eine Wand eingebundener Kamin in einem Wohnhof. Wand in Ziegelmauerwerk mit Feuerraum aus feuerfesten Steinen; Abschluß über Feuerraum und Holzlege aus Beton. Um den Kamin in den Hof zu integrieren, wurde davor eine kleine gemauerte Sitzgrube angelegt. (Wohnhaus in Udine, Italien, entworfen von Carlo Mangani.)

147

148, 149. Wall-incorporated fireplace in a living and dining room. Wall in brick masonry with firebox of firebricks; lintels of concrete. As protection against flying sparks, a grate has been fitted into the firebox which restricts the actual burning area to the rear part of the hearth. A large grill space is accommodated next to the fireplace. (Mogensen House, Hjarbaek Fjord, Denmark, designed by Børge Mogensen and Arne Karlsen.)

148, 149. In eine Wand eingebundener Kamin in einem Wohn- und Speiseraum. Wand in Ziegelmauerwerk mit Feuerraum aus feuerfesten Steinen; Stürze aus Beton. Zum Schutz gegen Funkenflug wird die Brennstelle durch ein Gitter auf den hinteren Teil des Feuertisches begrenzt. Neben dem Kamin befindet sich ein großer Grillplatz. (Haus Mogensen, Hjarbaek Fjord, Dänemark, entworfen von Børge Mogensen und Arne Karlsen.)

148

149

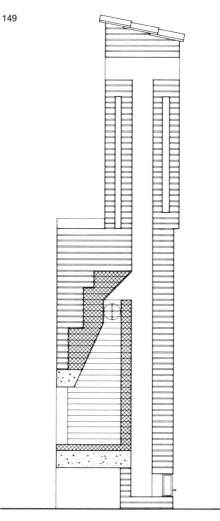

150. Wall-incorporated fireplace in a living room. Wall in brick masonry; continuing lintel above firebox and firewood niche of concrete; safety area of bricks. (Eddington House, Little Eversdon near Cambridge, England, designed by John Meunier.)

150. In eine Wand eingebundener Kamin in einem Wohnraum. Wand in Ziegelmauerwerk; durchlaufender Sturz über Feuerraum und Holzlege aus Beton; Sicherheitsstreifen aus Ziegelsteinen. (Eddington House, Little Eversdon bei Cambridge, England, entworfen von John Meunier.)

150

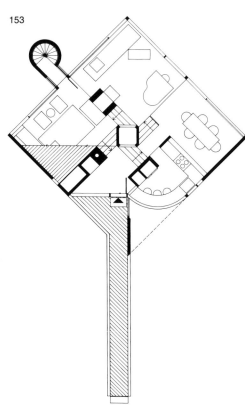

151–153. Freestanding fireplace between two living rooms. Fireplace block in brick masonry with intermediate slab of concrete; firebox lined with soapstone slabs; smoke flue of terra cotta with mantle of asbestos cement. The firebox opens to two sides and can be closed with metal-mesh curtains. On the lower plane, a firewood niche is accommodated beneath the firebox. (Simon Residence, Remsenburg, New York, designed by Julian Neski together with Barbara Neski and Ronald Bechtol.)

151–153. Frei stehender Kamin zwischen zwei Wohnräumen. Kaminblock in Ziegelmauerwerk mit Zwischenplatte aus Beton; Feuerraum mit Specksteinplatten ausgekleidet; Rauchrohr aus Terrakotta mit einem Mantel aus Asbestzement. Der Feuerraum ist nach zwei Seiten offen und kann durch Metallvorhänge verschlossen werden. Auf der unteren Ebene befindet sich unter dem Feuerraum eine Holzlege. (Simon Residence, Remsenburg, New York, entworfen von Julian Neski mit Barbara Neski und Ronald Bechtol.)

154. Wall-incorporated fireplace in a living room. Fireplace block in brick masonry with firebox of firebricks; smoke flue of brick elements, two-leaf, thermally insulated. The steel angle above the fireplace opening has been extended to protect the brickwork. A metal-mesh curtain eliminates the danger of flying sparks. (Residence in Essex Fells, New Jersey, designed by Richard Meier.)

154. In eine Wand eingebundener Kamin in einem Wohnraum. Kaminblock in Ziegelmauerwerk mit Feuerraum aus feuerfesten Steinen; Rauchrohr aus Ziegelelementen, zweischalig mit Wärmedämmung. Der Stahlwinkel über der Feueröffnung ist zum Schutz des Mauerwerks etwas vorgezogen. Funkenflug wird durch einen Metallvorhang vermieden. (Wohnhaus in Essex Fells, New Jersey, entworfen von Richard Meier.)

154

155–157. Fireplace sitting in front of a wall in a living room. Sub-structure in brickwork, faced with ceramic tiles, with firebox of fireclay bricks; smoke hood of steel plate lined with 1 cm thick asbestos sheets; hood facing of plaster, painted white; chimney in brickwork with concrete top. The fireplace is directly linked with the outside air through air ducts. The ash is collected in an ash drawer. (Martin House, Aiguafreda near Barcelona, designed by Emilio Donato and Uwe Geest.)

155–157. Vor einer Wand sitzender Kamin in einem Wohnraum. Unterkonstruktion in Mauerwerk, verkleidet mit Keramikplatten, mit Feuerraum aus Schamottesteinen; Rauchhaube aus Stahlblech, bekleidet mit 1 cm dicken Asbestplatten; Haubenverkleidung aus Putz, weiß gestrichen; Schornstein in Mauerwerk mit Kopf aus Beton. Der Kamin ist mit Zuluftkanälen direkt an die Außenluft angeschlossen. Die Asche wird in einer Aschenschublade gesammelt. (Haus Martin, Aiguafreda bei Barcelona, entworfen von Emilio Donato und Uwe Geest.)

155

156

157

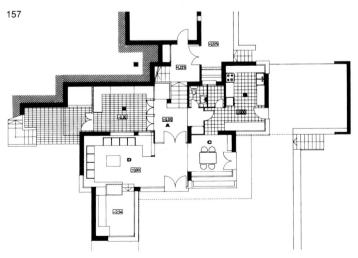

158. Fireplace incorporated in a bilaterally connected shelf and firewood niche construction, standing in front of a wall in a patio. Walls and chimney in brick masonry with firebox walls of fireclay bricks; floor slab, coverings and lintels of concrete; decorative stripes of „Puebla" tiles. (House in Cuernavaca, Mexico, designed by Karl-Heinz Götz.)

158. Vor einer Wand stehender Kamin in einem Wohnhof, eingebunden in eine beidseitig anschließende Ablage- und Holzlegekonstruktion. Wandstücke und Schornstein in Ziegelmauerwerk mit Feuerraumwänden aus Schamottesteinen; Bodenplatte, Abdeckungen und Stürze aus Beton; Zierstreifen aus „Puebla"-Kacheln. (Haus in Cuernavaca, Mexiko, entworfen von Karl-Heinz Götz.)

158

159

159. Freestanding fireplace in a living room. Fireplace construction in glazed-brick masonry with firebox of firebricks, painted black; cornice over the fireplace opening as steel angle, painted black; chimney lined with terra-cotta tiles. (Warner Residence, New Canaan, Connecticut, designed by John M. Johansen.)

159. Frei stehender Kamin in einem Wohnraum. Kaminkonstruktion in Mauerwerk aus glasierten Ziegeln mit Feuerraum aus feuerfesten Steinen, schwarz gestrichen; Sims über der Feueröffnung als Stahlwinkel, schwarz gestrichen; Schornstein mit Terrakottafliesen ausgekleidet. (Warner Residence, New Canaan, Connecticut, entworfen von John M. Johansen.)

160, 161. Freestanding fireplace in a living and dining room. Fireplace structure in brickwork, plastered; firebox as prefabricated element of light concrete, fireclay and cast iron (model „Superfire", type KNS, from the company Superpart AG, Bern); floor plate and cornice of concrete; smoke flue of prefabricated elements. The fireplace has a device for ash removal with collecting bin in the basement, over which air is simultaneously supplied to the fire. (Citron House, Carona, Switzerland, designed by Atelier 5.)

160, 161. Frei stehender Kamin in einem Wohn- und Speiseraum. Kaminkörper in Mauerwerk, verputzt; Feuerraum als Fertigteil aus Leichtbeton, Schamotte und Gußeisen (Modell „Superfire", Typ KNS, der Firma Superpart AG, Bern); Bodenplatte und Sims aus Beton; Rauchabzug aus Fertigteilen. Der Kamin verfügt über eine Aschenfallkonstruktion mit Sammelbehälter im Untergeschoß, die zugleich der Luftzufuhr dient. (Haus Citron, Carona, Schweiz, entworfen von Atelier 5.)

160

161

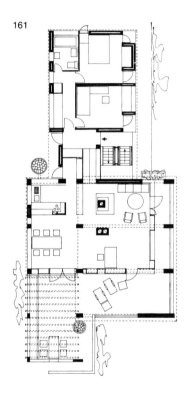

162, 163. Fireplace incorporated in a freestanding wall in a living and dining room. Wall and fireplace construction in brickwork, plastered (wall surfaces in rough-cast plaster, painted white, hood in smooth plaster, dark finish), with firebox of firebricks. This fireplace, like the one described previously, has a device for ash removal with collecting bin in the basement, over which air is simultaneously supplied to the fire. (House in a Paris suburb, designed by Michel Mortier.)

162, 163. In eine frei stehende Wand eingebundener Kamin in einem Wohn- und Speiseraum. Wand- und Kaminkonstruktion in Mauerwerk, verputzt (Wandflächen in weiß gestrichenem Rauhputz, Haube in dunkel gestrichenem Glattputz), mit Feuerraum aus feuerfesten Steinen. Wie der zuvor beschriebene Kamin verfügt auch dieser über eine Aschenfallkonstruktion mit Sammelbehälter im Untergeschoß, die zugleich der Luftzufuhr dient. (Haus in einem Vorort von Paris, entworfen von Michel Mortier.)

162

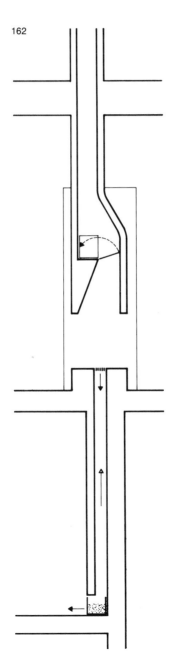

163

164. Wall-incorporated fireplace in a living room. Wall in masonry of large-sized light concrete blocks; hearth and back wall of firebricks; base and smoke hood of concrete; smoke flue of steel plate. The firebox is directly linked with the outside air; the fire burns on an iron grate with ash box below. The L-shaped bench of light concrete integrates the fireplace into the room. (House in Haddenham, England, designed by Peter J. Aldington.)

164. In eine Wand eingebundener Kamin in einem Wohnraum. Wand in Mauerwerk aus großformatigen Leichtbetonsteinen; Feuertisch und Feuerraumrückwand aus feuerfesten Ziegeln; Sockel und Rauchhaube aus Beton; Rauchrohr aus Stahlblech. Der Feuerraum ist direkt mit der Außenluft verbunden; das Feuer brennt auf einem Eisenrost, unter dem sich ein Aschenkasten befindet. Die L-förmige Sitzbank aus Leichtbetonsteinen bewirkt eine Integration des Kamins in das Raumgeschehen. (Haus in Haddenham, England, entworfen von Peter J. Aldington.)

164

165

165. Fireplace connected to a partition wall in a living and dining room; cheeks and wall in brick masonry with firebox of firebricks; base covered with ceramic tiles; smoke hood of steel plate; cornice of concrete; smoke flue of stainless steel, double-walled, with intermediate layer of asbestos. The fire burns on an iron grate and receives a direct supply of air from the exterior via a duct. (House in Histon near Cambridge, England, designed by David Thurlow.)

165. An eine Raumtrennwand angebundener Kamin in einem Wohn- und Speiseraum; Seitenwangen und Wand in Ziegelmauerwerk mit Feuerraum aus feuerfesten Steinen; Sockel mit Keramikfliesen belegt; Rauchhaube aus Stahlblech; Sims aus Beton; Rauchrohr aus Edelstahl, doppelwandig, mit Zwischenschicht aus Asbest. Das Feuer brennt auf einem Eisenrost und erhält über einen Kanal direkte Zuluft von außen. (Haus in Histon bei Cambridge, England, entworfen von David Thurlow.)

166

167

166. Wall-incorporated fireplace in a living room. Wall in brickwork, plastered; firebox of sandstone slabs; smoke hood of steel plate; beam over the fireplace opening of pine wood. The fire burns on an iron grate which can be lifted out for removal of ash. The fireplace is directly linked with the outside air via two ducts. (Borachia House, Albavilla near Como, designed by Vittorio Borachia.)

167. Wall-incorporated fireplace in a living room. Wall in brick masonry, plastered, with firebox of firebricks; base and cornice of terrazzo; lateral frames of stainless steel. (House in South Harting, England, designed by Stout & Litchfield.)

168. Wall-incorporated fireplace in a living room. Wall in brickwork, plastered, with firebox of firebricks; fireplace opening framed with marble. The fireplace receives direct supply air from the exterior. (Flat in Paris, designed by Alain Demachy.)

166. In eine Wand eingebundener Kamin in einem Wohnraum. Wand in Mauerwerk, verputzt; Feuerraum aus Sandsteinplatten; Rauchhaube aus Stahlblech; Balken über der Feuerraumöffnung aus Kiefernholz. Das Feuer brennt auf einem Eisenrost, der zum Entfernen der Asche abgenommen werden kann. Der Kamin ist über zwei Kanäle direkt mit der Außenluft verbunden. (Haus Borachia, Albavilla bei Como, entworfen von Vittorio Borachia.)

167. In eine Wand eingebundener Kamin in einem Wohnraum. Wand in Ziegelmauerwerk, verputzt, mit Feuerraum aus feuerfesten Steinen; Sockel und Sims aus Terrazzo; seitliche Profile aus Edelstahl. (Haus in South Harting, England, entworfen von Stout & Litchfield.)

168. In eine Wand eingebundener Kamin in einem Wohnraum. Wand in Mauerwerk, verputzt, mit Feuerraum aus feuerfesten Steinen; Rahmen um die Feueröffnung aus Marmor. Der Feuerraum erhält direkte Zuluft von außen. (Wohnung in Paris, entworfen von Alain Demachy.)

169–171. Fireplace sitting in front of a wall in a living room. Base in concrete; hearth and back wall of firebricks; smoke hood of enamelled steel; chimney as double-walled stainless-steel pipe standing free in front of the exterior wall. A metal-mesh screen running on a guide rail (not shown here) serves as spark guard. (Studebaker House, Mercer Island, Washington, designed by Wendell H. Lovett.)

169–171. Vor einer Wand sitzender Kamin in einem Wohnraum. Sockel in Beton; Feuertisch und Rückwand aus feuerfesten Ziegeln; Rauchhaube aus Stahlblech, gestrichen; Schornstein als frei vor der Außenwand stehendes doppelwandiges Edelstahlrohr. Als Funkenschutz dient ein in einer Schiene laufender, hier nicht gezeigter Metallvorhang. (Studebaker House, Mercer Island, Washington, entworfen von Wendell H. Lovett.)

169

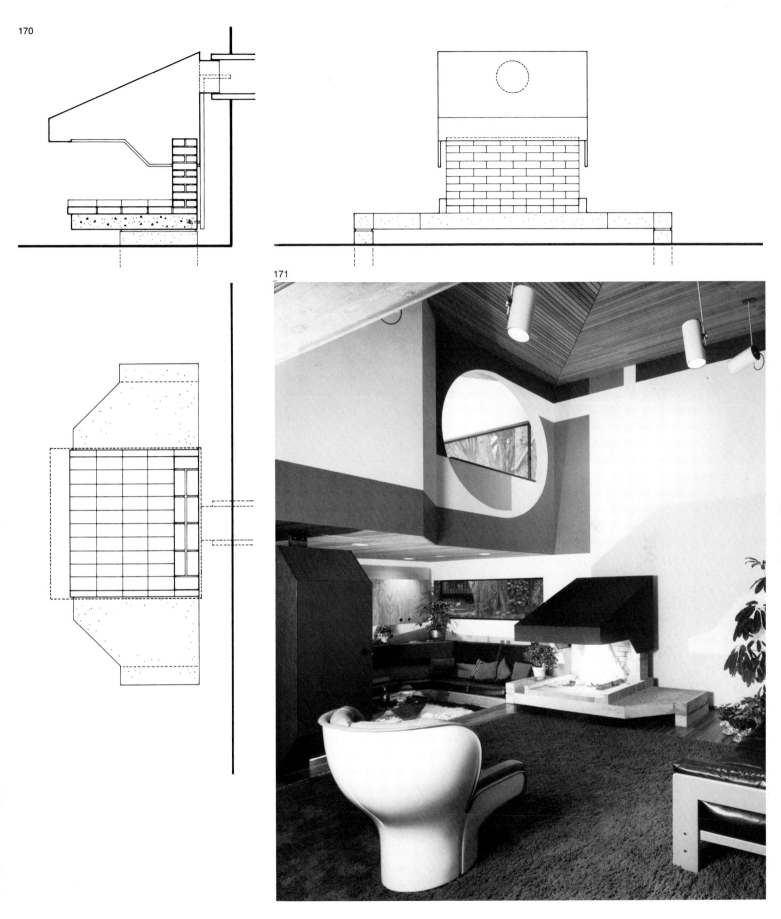

172–175. Fireplace incorporated in a parapet in a living room. Lateral wall sheets in concrete-block masonry; fireplace structure in brick masonry, plastered; firebox lined with fire-bricks; smoke flue as prefabricated concrete element, painted; coping stone over the fireplace structure of poured concrete. Top and sides of the fireplace opening framed with steel angles; the lateral angles are arranged in such a way that they cover the interfaces of the fireproof lining. (Gissing House, Wahroonga, Australia, designed by Harry Seidler & Associates.)

172–175. In eine Brüstung eingebundener Kamin in einem Wohnraum. Seitliche Wandscheiben in Betonsteinmauerwerk; Kaminkörper in Ziegelmauerwerk, verputzt; Feuerraum mit feuerfesten Steinen ausgekleidet; Rauchrohr als Betonfertigteil, gestrichen; Abdeckplatte über dem Kaminkörper aus Ortbeton. Die Feuerraumöffnung ist seitlich und oben mit Stahlwinkeln eingefaßt; die seitlichen Winkel sind so angeordnet, daß sie die Stirnseiten der feuerfesten Auskleidung abdecken. (Gissing House, Wahroonga, Australien, entworfen von Harry Seidler & Associates.)

172

173

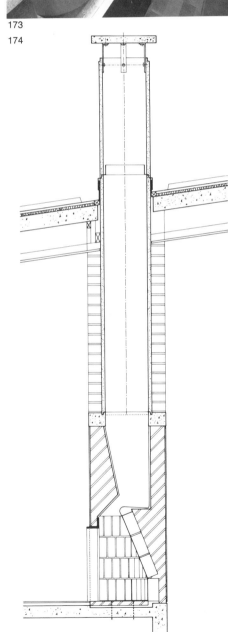

174

175

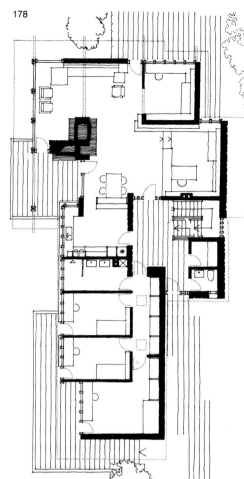

177

176–178. Combination fireplace with fireboxes in a living room and on a terrace. Base and wall parts in sandstone masonry; fireboxes lined with firebricks; beam of oak wood; smoke hoods in plastered brickwork. Since the house is located on a hillside with frequently occuring downwinds, an electric ventilator was installed on the chimney top in order to guarantee sufficient draught. (Villa Jean Weill, Obernais, France, designed by René Heller and Bertel Udsen.)

176–178. Kombinationskamin mit Feuerstellen in einem Wohnraum und an einem Freiplatz. Sockel und Wandstücke in Sandsteinmauerwerk; Feuerräume mit feuerfesten Ziegeln ausgekleidet; Balken aus Eichenholz; Rauchhauben in Mauerwerk, verputzt. Da das Haus an einem Hang mit häufig auftretenden Fallwinden liegt, wurde auf dem Schornsteinkopf ein elektrischer Ventilator installiert, um in jedem Fall eine ausreichende Zugleistung zu gewährleisten. (Villa Jean Weill, Obernais, Frankreich, entworfen von René Heller und Bertel Udsen.)

179. Fireplace incorporated in an exterior wall in a living room. Fireplace structure in natural-stone masonry; lintel of concrete; plastered wall above the lintel; chimney lining of clay. (House in Somerton, England, designed by Stout & Litchfield.)

179. In eine Außenwand eingebundener Kamin in einem Wohnraum. Kaminkörper in Natursteinmauerwerk; Sturz aus Beton; Wand über dem Sturz verputzt; Schornsteinauskleidung aus Ton. (Haus in Somerton, England, entworfen von Stout & Litchfield.)

179

## Architects, designers, manufacturers
## Architekten, Entwerfer, Hersteller

**Photographers / Photographen**